NETWORKING

FOR

AUTHORS

How to Make Friends, Sell More Books and Grow a Publishing Network from Scratch

DAN PARSONS

Networking for Authors
How to Make Friends, Sell More Books and Grow a Publishing Network
from Scratch

First Edition 2020

ISBN: 978-1-913564-00-1

Category: Business & Economics / Entrepreneurship / Networking

Contents

Acknowledgements

As an author, you don't often realise how many people have helped you create a book until you really think about it. When that book also happens to be about networking, that list of names becomes unmanageably large. As a result, I'll try to be as brief as possible without leaving out anyone who played a vital role.

Of course, I must start with my family. My parents, in particular, have always supported my writing obsession. Plus, my uncle, Colin R. Parsons, should also get a mention for being the first author I knew, even before either of us had any connections.

Then there's my team: my editor David Norrington at Wordcatcher Publishing; my cover designer on this project, Stuart Bache; and my proofreader, Joe Moore. On top of that, there's my audiobook producer, Mark Chatterley, at In Ear Entertainment and J D Kelly, who is the talented voice actor behind the audiobook version of *Networking for Authors*. All are swift, thorough and professional.

My childhood friends, Nathan Smith and poet Philip John, must also be thanked. Both have followed my author career since it started and frequently help me make decisions on everything from initial ideas to cover design.

Then there are all of the author-friends and book trade professionals who make up my network. It is their time, generosity and experiences that have made this book possible. Their presence has seriously improved my career and the quality of my life. Some of you have had a direct involvement in the creation of *Networking for Authors*. Others have appeared in case studies. Whether I know you from an online group or in the real world, as a close contact or a friend of a friend, you have provided more help than you realise.

In no particular order, just a few notable names include: Sacha Black, Adam Croft, Michael John Grist, Mark Dawson, James Blatch, Tom Ashford, Elaine Bateman, Jon Evans, Steven Moore, Zoe Foster, Andy Peloquin, Joanna Penn, Orna Ross, Michael Anderle, Craig Martelle, David Penny, Kinga Jentetics, Dan Woods, Rachel Abbot, L J Shen, Darren Hassall, Justin Sloan, Amanda M. Lee and Chris Fox. Together, you make the publishing community a magical place to be.

No doubt I've missed some critical names and I won't realise until this book goes to print, but that's the nature of publishing. Thankfully, my network is full of good people so we will remain firm friends.

Introduction

So, you're an author. One of many. There are at least four million of us in total. If you come from a community where writing books isn't the norm, that stat might seem unlikely. However, it's true, according to Amazon's author ranks, which lists all known authors on their database from best to worst sellers. And that's not including the ones that have never been uploaded.

Many ordinary, non-writing folk imagine authors as "special" individuals – a different breed of human, born with talent and connections. Even the late, mega-bestselling fantasy author Terry Pratchett once admitted in an interview that, at a young age, he believed he would never become one because that didn't happen to people like *him*. He didn't have a fancy degree, nor did he come from a long line of famous writers. He knew nobody in publishing.

Then he met an author at a literary event and made a surprising discovery: authors are normal people. They spend more time writing than others but they share the same biology. They have the same fears and insecurities. Some are lazy. Some work hard. Some are born into upper-class families and some are working class. They aren't innately special. Who they were didn't make them authors. It's what they did that got them there. Being an author is something that's earned, not an identity you're given at birth.

If you're new to the industry, you possibly feel like Young Terry: daunted. Luckily, that's about to change. Whether you're writing a book or have a dozen published, this book is for you.

Its purpose is to open your eyes to the opportunities that become available when you start networking, and to give you the skills to capitalise on them and change your life.

Some of the topics it covers include how to:

- Identify ways in which networking can benefit you
- Find and compare the best places to meet other writers
- Build an author network from scratch
- Work out which contacts make good connections
- Overcome shyness and technophobia
- Find relevant industry connections online
- Strengthen relationships without leaving home
- Meet contacts in the real world
- Mentally and practically prepare for a physical event
- Maximise your networking efforts at conferences
- Get invited to afterparties and private side events
- Enter conversations at parties to meet more people
- Turn contacts into real friends in just a few hours
- Create lasting bonds at conferences
- Be remembered beyond your first introduction
- Deepen long-term relationships
- Build your networking momentum
- Gain the respect of your publishing peers
- Establish a network that will last your entire career
- Create opportunities for future authors
- Leave a legacy and be remembered

Will this guide help you write your book? No.

Will it help you market your book? Indirectly, but that's not why you're here.

This book won't make you a bestseller by itself. But it will help you establish yourself as an active figure in the author community and allow you to build a network of powerful, professional friends who can help you get ahead in your writing career.

Throughout the course of this book, I will explore some universal networking techniques that can be used by writers making a living from a variety of disciplines. This is because modern authors have varied business models. Some make a full-time income from book sales alone. Others have more diverse ways of supplementing income for their author business, from helping to design other authors' book covers to podcasting their journeys as writers.

I include financial figures to demonstrate exactly how much the authors featured in the case studies have benefited from different tactics. Although I am a British author, the primary currency mentioned will be US dollars. This is because, while authors live in every territory and books are sold in every currency, many of the best reports and case studies come from US sources. Likewise, most of the best industry tools on the market have been created by US companies or focus on the US. Having said that, the concepts we explore will have universal appeal for authors around the globe. The US dollar is simply a constant that most authors recognise as a benchmark.

Continuing the focus on transparency, many of the conversations discussed in this book contain the real names of friends, authors in case studies, and those I consider mentors. Where personal information has been shared, some names have been omitted. If the information has never been mentioned in a public broadcast or could be considered controversial, I have kept the speaker anonymous to save them from criticism.

As for me, I try to be as candid as possible. Allow me to introduce myself. My name is Daniel Parsons and I'm the author of eight books, three of which have made it onto bestseller lists in the US, UK, Canada and Australia. During my professional career, I have worked for three traditional publishing companies, as a production assistant, editor, proofreader and marketing executive. I've also managed two bookstores, one indie and the other a branch of a national chain. My books have been read in 70 countries and have been used in the marketing campaign for Hollywood's *Pride and Prejudice and Zombies* movie.

While I'm not quite a Pratchett – I don't have legions of fans and worldwide tours – I would consider myself a relatively well-connected author with enough success to call myself professional. I am an indie author. That means I'm self-published and plan to stay that way unless the right publisher makes me an offer I can't refuse.

For this reason, this book won't be centred around schmoozing agents and publishers to secure yourself a deal. Negotiating with them will come up but it won't be the main focus. The primary focus is in helping you to build a strong, comprehensive network of your own: collaborators, marketers, agents, editors, cover designers, publishers, distributors and whoever else will strengthen your position.

Our mantra won't be to craft a spectacular book and wait around for it to get picked up by someone with power and connections. It will be to *become* that person with power and connections. To give yourself the power of a publisher, even if you want to be traditionally published. In short, the book will give you options.

If you're new to the industry, you won't necessarily know exactly how it works. How publishers used to hold most of the power and how the internet has slowly placed more of that power into authors' hands. Don't worry. When I started my writing career, I didn't know any of this either. Thankfully, I've learned a lot due to the conversations I had while networking.

To give you some context, online I have dozens of author and publisher friends who I chat with on a daily basis, plus hundreds more who I talk to on a less regular basis – and that's not counting my 80,000+ Twitter followers.

Offline, I'm well-rooted in my country's writing community too. In South Wales, UK, where I live, I personally know a ton of local authors. I've helped run a book fair and I've spoken at events. I often bump into author-friends at bookstores and local fairs.

The same goes for further afield, almost 200 miles away in London, where I frequent the UK's biggest annual publishing conference. While there, I'm almost never alone, surrounded by authors, podcasters, distributors and editors, with whom I grab coffee and share pizzas. In the bars around the venue, someone almost always spots me and waves in recognition – including some I once revered as idols.

I've made lifelong friends and gained valuable advantages as a result of these relationships. I'm not saying any of this to brag. I'm simply showing you that it's possible to create strong bonds in a community, even if you start out a stranger.

Back in 2013, I knew nobody. I was a newbie author, unpublished and yet to work for any publishers or booksellers. All I had was a dream of becoming a bestseller. There was a lot of enthusiasm, but I couldn't act on it effectively because I lacked guidance from anyone who knew what they were doing.

My immediate family weren't creatives. I had an uncle who was also a new writer, but at the time, he was just as unconnected as me, yet to find success as a children's author under the name Colin R. Parsons. Everyone else in my life were ordinary, practical people. They worked nine-to-fives and spent their weekends watching TV or hanging out with friends. None of my friends understood why anyone would shrug off the idea of a "real job" and give up their free time to tap away at a laptop.

When I was writing, they said frustrating things like:

"As you're not doing anything, could you help me move a wardrobe?"

"Writing a book, are you? I'd do that if I had the time." (No, they wouldn't.)

"Why are you wasting your time? Settle on a normal job and work your way up like everyone else!"

"You know most writers don't make any money, right? You're born into something like that."

Sounds familiar? As I mentioned, the world contains four million published authors. Yet, with seven billion people living in the world, that still means less than one in a thousand will understand this struggle.

When you start out, it can seem like you're alone. This book will help you surround yourself with so many like minds it'll feel like everyone and their poodle is writing a book. Don't be intimidated though, because knowledge is more powerful than ignorance. Being able to see who's beating your best efforts also means being able to adapt based on what you learn. Plus, if you know them personally, then they'll know you, and that can only be good for your reputation.

To illustrate my point, in early 2019, a fellow zombie author, Michael John Grist, dropped me an email. We met at a book fair in 2016 and have been comparing tactics ever since. In his latest email, he told me that he had been at a networking event. While there, writing non-fiction had come up in conversation, along with my name. It turned out, a few of the attendees were familiar with me and started talking about my upcoming non-fiction release.

I wasn't a part of this party and yet here I was, being discussed – and in a good way! Authors who didn't know me were hearing my name as a point of interest. Do you think that name-drop led to an opportunity? You bet! Off the back of that conversation, two authors contacted me, one asking for a copy to review and the other letting me know I could promote it by being interviewed on their podcast.

In publishing, reputation goes a long way. It can get you invited to contribute to anthologies, or valuable marketing opportunities. It can help you talk your way into private functions. It can also get you a publishing deal.

I'm not saying this book will get you everywhere. There are limits. After all, I'm not Tony Robbins or Stephen King (yet). I don't break bread with movie producers or rub shoulders with billionaires. But if I did, this book wouldn't be of much use to you because you couldn't replicate such tactics.

The best way to reach a higher plateau is to take advice from someone who recently got there and is enjoying the view.

Someone who has spent decades at the mountaintop might not remember the path they took to get there. How they did so 30 years ago might not even be possible now. Or new developments in technology might mean that there's an easier way.

I won't disregard advice from the legends of publishing. There will be anecdotes drawn from personal experiences that have worked well for me but there will also be stats and research to back up that advice. We will look into psychology, technological trends and established business practices and draw conclusions specifically for writers.

I have also cherrypicked advice from interviews and personal conversations with a host of rising author megastars, as well as blog posts and speaking engagements. Every rock has been turned to make this the best networking book for new writers or those simply inexperienced at networking.

The rules have changed, but stratospheric success and glamourous connections *are* achievable. It just takes baby steps. At first, that might mean simply talking to one or two authors on social media. The next step would entail going to a local book signing, or a workshop. Then, eventually, a bustling publishing conference.

Each chapter will guide you a little further outside your comfort zone. Sections 1-4 will start by defining networking, demonstrating its benefits and what you can achieve. Sections 5-7 will outline a guide to networking online, which will be the starting place for most people. In sections 8-13, we will move to networking in the real world. Then 14-16 will go into detail about mixing both strategies to achieve the best results. If you only want to learn about one topic, you can skip forward using the contents.

I break down each section into easy-to-manage actions that can be carried out at your own pace. Don't worry about being unprepared. Everyone feels that way at first. It means you're growing. There's no need to panic because every chapter ends with a cheat-sheet that you can use to recap, even seconds before entering a room.

You don't need to know everyone, just the *right* people. The people who "get" you. This book will give you the framework to reach those people – your tribe. And when you get there, it will help you make the most of that tight-knit team and use collaborations as a platform upon which to build your reputation.

Reading this book, you will learn:

1. What networking is and isn't, to give you a clear idea of what you need to achieve
2. Why you *should* network and the benefits that will follow if you do it well
3. How to network if you're a technophobe, an introvert, or both
4. How to find your tribe and connect with them effectively using the internet
5. The art of getting attention and establishing your presence without committing social *faux pas*
6. How to nurture strong virtual relationships with people you have never met in the real world
7. The best ways to build a reputation as a pillar of the online writing community
8. Why physical networking builds a lasting network of trusted, professional friends

9. Mantras for tackling stressful pre-event concerns
10. Actionable tactics you can run through to prepare for an event
11. How to convert complete strangers into contacts and even friends in one meeting
12. Troubleshooting tips if you find yourself turning into a wallflower
13. Ways to get your network to spread your reputation and get you opportunities without you being present
14. A game plan for lasting long term as a connector
15. A guide to keeping the publishing ecosystem diverse to protect your business and the industry you love
16. How to position yourself as the go-to contact for new writers set to become the titans of tomorrow

As you can see, this book will take you on a journey from a complete novice, spreading your feelers into the unknown, to a connected professional with deep, powerful friendships across the globe.

I
WHAT IS NETWORKING?

Lesson 101. At first glance, defining networking seems easy:

It's schmoozing! It's sucking up to people who can get you what you want. It's knowing everyone and how to get something out of them.

Right? Wrong. Sucking up or manipulating people is what many newbies think are effective strategies, but the truth is they won't serve you for long. Networking is more about giving than receiving. To explain this, it's best to demonstrate bad networking first.

NETWORKING IS NOT...

Firstly, it's not sucking up. You can leave the sleaze to phoney marketing gurus and that guy in every gangster movie who pleads for his life before getting his head blown off. It doesn't work. It just makes you look desperate and sets off strangers' alarm bells. It makes people wonder what you *really* want, which is no way to make friends.

Another thing that networking isn't, is doing *everything* for "exposure" instead of payment. This might seem like an age-old rite of passage but the myth of exposure has been... ahem... exposed.

You know the drill: you attend a ticket-charging event, give a speech and help to promote the event in return for... not much, really. A side room containing ten vaguely interested strangers. In recent decades, this exposure idea has provided a crutch for organisers to attract numbers and bolster profits, exploiting free labour in the name of a leg-up. It's an unpaid internship. But attending one event doesn't necessarily make you any more likely to get booked for a bigger, paid gig.

> "Come and speak for us. It'll give you a lot of exposure. Are we charging for the event? Absolutely! Are we paying you? Yes... with *opportunities*."

This exposure is often over-hyped and isn't worth your time or effort. Thanks to a movement started by author Philip Pullman, however, things are changing. Currently, this exploitative practice is considered disrespectful, with many professional authors boycotting non-paying literary festivals that charge for entry. The general sentiment among professional writers is that "authors die of exposure."

It devalues your time and often leads to underwhelming rewards. The average number of books sold per author is generally small at all but the biggest festivals, and many don't provide enough promotional opportunities to justify travel expenses.

Put simply, if you've written a book and are considered an expert worthy of speaking at a ticketed event, you should get paid.

Fair enough if the event is free for visitors. If you want to help a community event, that's honourable and great for the town. Not every event organiser is a predator. Many amateur organisers genuinely don't have the budgets and *believe* their offer will help authors. But that isn't always the case.

Either way, predator or well-meaning community pillar, these gigs will almost certainly provide less value to your career than spending a few hours writing or marketing online.

That's not to say there aren't exceptions. A national TV show appearance *can* boost your reputation and lead to high-profile contacts. Likewise, if you're a non-fiction author who also sells courses, unpaid speaking gigs work as lead-generation to draw in clients.

Working for "exposure" and sucking-up to powerful figures are two tactics newbie authors think are good networking tactics when, in fact, they lead to little. So, if those practices aren't good networking, what is?

Networking Is...

The most basic definition of effective networking is:

Communicating with strength,
respect and an eye for opportunities.

See how that definition fundamentally differs from the previous one? Both parties approach the table as equals, looking for mutual benefits, and both can walk away at any time with their dignity.

It removes the idea that *real* writers don't or shouldn't network and empowers authors to take part in productive conversations. It encourages them to avoid the "starving artist" archetype and take responsibility for furthering their own career, either in collaboration with their publisher or as an independent author.

Networking is making a conscious effort to build you own power and influence. That way, you don't *need* to be "picked up" by a publisher who will handle the business side of things. You can either build your own independent empire or kickstart your career to attract publishers. It gives you options. No more waiting for a lucky break. You create your own luck. Thanks to the internet, it's easier than ever, no matter your social background.

In modern publishing, the old adage, "It's not what you know, it's who you know," doesn't necessarily apply. Anyone can self-publish, advertise their book and distribute globally. I've seen authors turn up at networking events one year, completely unpublished with no contacts. The next year, they've transformed themselves into rock-star bestsellers with a dozen titles and a full-time writing income.

Nepotism is slowly being replaced by meritocracy. The most talented, hardest workers rise to the top. However, we don't live in a utopia yet.

At one point in history there were people called gatekeepers – agents, publishers, bookstore buyers – people who curated the books that got published and exposed to readers. Writers had to prove themselves to these people and sometimes sign contracts that weighed heavily in the publishers' favour. This has changed, but the need for publishing professionals hasn't gone away. Indeed, there are some excellent publishers that champion their authors, proactively providing value and getting opportunities for those who would struggle without help.

On the flipside, there are also more choices than ever for authors to back themselves. Yet, as an indie author, you can't do everything alone.

Nowadays, the biggest problem isn't getting your next book published. As a lot of writers are now publishers, they no longer need help in that department. Instead, the competitive focus of author networking has shifted to solve problems experienced by the publishers themselves.

Major issues writers look to fix today include increasing production quality, finding new marketplaces where their work can thrive, and looking for collaborative opportunities. The biggest theme overarching these problems is that writers in this crowded marketplace have to stand out.

If you haven't published a book yet, this shouldn't be your networking priority. It should be finding supportive writers to help you finish your book. However, building a long-term strategy for exposure into your networking plan is easier than applying it after the fact, so always keep that in mind.

An efficient way to do this is to build friendships among the major ebook vendors – Amazon, Kobo, Google Play and Apple Books. Reps can get your work in front of thousands, if not millions of readers. However, in a true Catch-22 scenario, to get their help you first need to pique their interest with strong initial sales. Weirdly, this caveat works in your favour.

This is because the best way to network is to enter discussions with the confidence to walk away without a deal.

That way, you're not grovelling for a favour: you're showing you have something to offer them if they want to get involved. By not being able to enter a deal until you've already mastered marketing and built a strong reputation on your own, you are stopped from taking a bad deal and derailing your progress, simply because you no longer need it to survive.

For example, if you approach a rep with an untested book, buy them a drink and ask them to promote your book, you'll probably strike out. That's a good thing because, in that situation, they hold all the power and can demand pretty much whatever they want, knowing how much the deal could help you progress. On the other hand, if you approach them with a solid sales history and a plan, they will be more inclined to take you seriously and respect you.

Say you've got a book that suits its genre perfectly. You've had it professionally edited, the cover resonates with readers, it has a captivating product page, fantastic reviews and a strong sales history. You've got an attractive product.

Knowing this, you can offer a retail rep the chance to have you next book exclusively on their platform for its official launch week. That way, they have something unique to offer their readers. In exchange, you ask them to promote your book on the front page of their website for that launch week, allowing you to dominate the genre.

See how that's a better scenario? You already have a great book and you don't *need* this person to get involved because you can make your book a success on your own or approach a competitor. This power *saves* you from entering a bad deal.

If the rep still decides your book isn't for them, that's fine. Move on and ask someone else. Nobody in this situation is desperate and nobody is asking for a favour. Both parties would be benefiting from the collaboration. It's a win-win. That's networking.

Hugh Howey, popular author of the *Wool* trilogy, is a perfect example of using this style of networking to advance his career. In 2013, Howey found unexpected fame when his self-published book *Wool* hit the *New York Times* bestseller list and, according to the *Writer's Digest*, his royalty payments ballooned to $150,000 a month on ebook sales alone. Noticing his success, huge publishers approached him. Their one condition was that they wanted the rights to his books in all formats.

Already maximising his ebook potential, Howey reasoned that they had nothing to offer him in that area so negotiated for a print-only deal. He even turned down a seven-figure offer, complete with full bookstore distribution. It was only when *Simon & Shuster* offered him the mid-six-figure print-only deal he wanted that he finally agreed to work with them.

At the time, no doubt, it would have been tempting to take publishers' earlier offers – to play in the traditional publishing space. A seven-figure advance and your book in the front of every major bookshop is the dream for many. However, Howey knew that it wasn't the right deal for him, so he didn't waver. As much as he might have wanted to become a member of the New York publishing social elite, he knew he had a hot product to offer and wouldn't sell himself short to join them.

If you don't have a book yet, your networking will look different to Howey's but the dynamic will be the same. You might offer another writer a story critique in exchange for them keeping you accountable for your daily wordcount goals. Or you could offer to take a chance on a newbie cover designer at a reduced rate. They get a testimonial from a real author and get paid, you get a cover.

Notice that in these cases you give something rather than just taking? In some cases, you give more value than you receive. That's because networking is about being generous, not trying to control others. Influencing other people's opinions about you so they take action in your favour is preferable to begging or coercing.

Some of the best networking I've done has come from helping someone and not asking for anything in return. Sounds crazy, right? It doesn't always work, but if you help enough people, some of them *will* volunteer to help you later. In some cases, you won't even have to ask.

And this principle is backed up by numerous academics, including Robert B. Cialdini in his landmark book *Influence: The Psychology of Persuasion*. According to Cialdini, when it comes to human psychology, "There is an obligation to give, an obligation to receive and an obligation to repay."

This approach makes perfect sense in creative industries like publishing and music. Making ambitious projects successful requires lots of skills. Not everyone can write a great plot, or edit until it sparkles, or create a striking cover, or market it using online video, or manage advertising. Each step requires a different type of artistry and you can't master every skill or always afford to pay someone to do those things for you. But you can work with those who already have those skills.

Good networking teaches you that you always have value to someone. Collaborate enough and you can build an entity that, as a whole, is greater than the sum of its parts. It's about building a robust web of collaborators and supporters that can help you complete your projects without having to rely entirely on any one powerful individual.

Successful artists these days don't join brands – they become brands. They know it keeps the power in their hands, so they own it, meaning they don't have to answer to anyone. It vindicates them to reinvent their art and business in whatever way they choose, unimpeded by anyone.

Increasingly, people are also turning themselves into brands to bolster their personal reputation, rather than that of their company. That way, they can attract people who want to work with *them*, even if they close or sell that company.

In his book, *Youpreneur*, serial entrepreneur Chris Ducker talks about becoming a go-to leader in any industry he inhabits. It futureproofs his career. And he's not the only one. Becoming a "youpreneur" is a movement that's spreading into every crevice of society. Influencers are everywhere, led by the Kardashian family whose personal brand has turned idea after idea into cash cows. Not everyone admires their lifestyle, but they must acknowledge their global clout.

If building an influencer brand sounds harder than being picked up, feel free to keep looking for the big break you dreamed of as a child. Or buy lottery tickets. Both *could* happen but are far from guaranteed.

If you *are* interested in pursuing this definition of networking success – one that is more likely to grant you more long-term progress – read on to see a selection of its potential benefits. And remember, this is only the surface. Beneath lies a goldmine of opportunities.

Quick Takeaways

Networking as an author, means:

Do Not

- ✗ suck up to people in positions of power
- ✗ work unpaid at profitable events
- ✗ seek "exposure" as the sole reward for participating in a ticketed event
- ✗ expect immediate payback

Do

- ✓ communicate from a position of strength
- ✓ build your own power and influence rather than relying on being "picked up"
- ✓ use the internet to reach your tribe
- ✓ help others to build a professional rapport
- ✓ make ethical deals in which both you and the other person can simply walk away
- ✓ become part of a supportive writing community
- ✓ build your own connections instead of relying on a publisher
- ✓ talk to a diverse range of professionals
- ✓ learn new skills until you have something to offer
- ✓ trade expertise
- ✓ cheerlead for your fellow newbies
- ✓ become a brand so success will follow you to new business ideas
- ✓ futureproof your process so you always have someone to turn to if a connection disappears

2
Benefits of Networking

Networking has a cocktail of potential benefits. The aim of this chapter is to show you exactly what mastering it can help you achieve.

There are examples everywhere of fantastic networking prowess. The two authors whose stories we are about to explore are both great writers. However, their success hasn't stemmed purely from writing stunning prose. They are also notable networkers. Potentially, luck plays a part too, but success born of luck is often short-lived. What these two authors have demonstrated is a remarkable talent for acquiring diehard supporters, a knack that has given them long-term success.

What Can Be Achieved — Case Studies

Hugh Howey is one of independent publishing's legendary success stories who broke out during the 2011 Kindle gold rush – a time when the Kindle took off, reader demand for ebooks was high, and few authors knew how to self-publish and fulfil that demand. While others who shared in this success faded, he continued to publish successfully.

Interestingly, the reason for his longevity is apparent from the stories told by authors who have encountered him. Research him and you will see similar descriptions crop up across the board: generous, helpful and friendly. Therefore, when you consider Howey's initial book launches (which were characterised by writer-friends swarming to help him) the link between his relationship-building prowess and his success makes sense.

He's a posterchild for networking. He started by being eager to help and be useful to other writers long before releasing his first book. As a result, the seeds he planted bore a bounty of fruit. He's sold millions of books and has received seven-figure offers, as well as a movie deal.

Romance author L J Shen has become similarly accomplished. In contemporary romance – one of the most lucrative and, therefore, competitive fiction genres – Shen holds her own against the likes of Nora Roberts, Danielle Steel and Jo Jo Moyes without the backing of a large, traditional publisher.

Shen first drew my attention in early 2019 when she released her eleventh book, *The Kiss Thief*. By that point, it had amassed 1,400 mostly glowing reviews and had not left the top 20 Kindle bestsellers for a month. Pretty impressive, considering her biggest competitors were struggling to garner 300 reviews and stay a bestseller for more than a week.

Upon discovering this phenomenal launch, I immediately investigated, asking if anyone in a Facebook group of more than 20,000 authors knew what she had done to see such stellar results. What I found astounded me. Authors who knew Shen responded quickly with gushing praise, saying she was a great writer but also that they felt a powerful connection with her.

The common theme among their comments was that she was a "rock star" in the romance community. Her success was due to more than her books. As much as these authors wanted to analyse her as professionals, they couldn't help but rave, jostling to be crowned her number one fan. There were comments about the enthusiastic way she treats other authors but the real gem in her PR crown was her fan service. She *gave* so much to her fans that they felt like personal friends.

Shen ran a super-active Facebook group, comprising of authors and readers alike, and responded to comments personally, even if there were hundreds. She was open to their ideas, time permitting, and shared glimpses of her works-in-progress. She wasn't an entirely open book, but she did treat her fans and colleagues like real friends, regardless of whether they'd ever met. Due to this personal touch, they gushed about her work to anyone who would listen.

It wasn't long before I saw this PR masterclass in action. Within hours of my original question there were murmurs in the comments claiming that she had heard she was being discussed. Even her emotion was conveyed for her, her fans acting like messengers: she was thrilled and humbled.

I immediately felt the power of her network envelop me, everyone somehow sticking to an unspoken script that kept her reputation perfectly on brand. Somehow, her presence had become palpable without her ever having to join the group.

At the same time, James Blatch, who is a successful podcaster in this space, chimed in on my conversation. In response to the interest, he had reached out to ask her some questions. As he was well known in the industry, he offered her a public interview, which he would publish on his blog. Despite not needing to do this (she is already undoubtedly a millionaire and we weren't her target readership) she agreed to answer questions crowdsourced by the group. She answered them with real thought and candour.

There are two major lessons in this case study:

1. Would I have managed to get a million-selling, rock-star author to answer a series of probing questions about her marketing process alone? No. Not without the power of the group and my podcaster connection.
2. Shen's consistent, unwavering generosity tells us that being generous to *everyone*, even if they're outside your readership, is worthwhile.

There's a reason why readers *and* authors love her. Shen's always giving and she doesn't discriminate. In most cases, writers view talking to potential or existing readers as marketing. It's a linear sales funnel – a process in which they transform browsers into readers, readers into fans and fans into super-fans. Shen's tactic works more like a nebulous cloud. She draws strangers into her gravitational field, attracting them by providing value, even if there isn't an obvious payoff. This leads to unexpected opportunities, like gaining respect among authors outside her genre and potentially being offered paid speaking gigs at writers' conferences.

In this industry, there's a concept called a "launch team" – a select group of fans invited by an author to join a reading club to read an Advance Reader Copy (ARC). The deal is this: the author gives these true fans ARCs of their upcoming releases for free. In return, these fans read and review the book before launch week so the author has some social proof to help their marketing.

Most midlist writers – those who sell enough books to support a moderate lifestyle but don't publish huge bestsellers – have around 100 members and will get 10-80 reviews during launch week, depending on their team's engagement level. Some more established authors have 300-500 ARC readers and can get 200+ reviews during launch.

Do you know how many ARC readers L J Shen has? Only 100 – and yet she gets well over 1,000 reviews per book! That's because she has cultivated her launch team into a slick networking operation. Each member goes beyond their ordinary launch team duties. As super-fans, besides leaving reviews, they spread the word and get their friends involved, not because of some pyramid scheme or commission incentive masterminded by Shen but because they genuinely want to help.

This book isn't about book launches. That's a different topic. It's about making *professional* connections, so the majority of the chapters will be dedicated to attaining that goal. This second case study is worth noting, though, because it opens your eyes to the possibilities of approaching networking with creative flair.

MAKE GENUINE FRIENDS

Now that you've seen the dizzying potential of networking at the top level, let's get back to the basics. In its simplest form, networking creates friendships. Writing, for most authors, is a solitary job. As writers, we spend a lot of time in our own heads, creating worlds and devising plot twists, commonly opting for silence or headphones.

Some make frequent trips to coffee shops or share office spaces for background noise. Others write in groups to keep from going insane. But these aren't options for everyone. Some writers can't afford to chain-drink overpriced coffees and others need distraction-free concentration to get anything done. Under such circumstances, the writing life can become lonely.

Networking gives writers a chance to meet peers who understand their lifestyle and struggles. Studies reported everywhere from the *New York Times* to *Scientific American* suggest that humanity, as a sociable species, needs interaction to maintain a good state of mental health. It's also known that most people respond best to those who share common interests. Those who display the greatest level of job satisfaction aren't those who love what they do – although that helps. It's those who get on with their colleagues. According to Gretchen Rubin's book, *The Happiness Project*, having co-workers you like is *the* most important factor for professional happiness.

If you've ever been in a room full of writers, you'll feel the buzz of enthusiasm, ideas and advice. Writers bond over relatable woes and encourage each other to keep going. They share the same dream and know the importance of cheering on their friends, having perhaps lacked similar encouragement elsewhere. Many leave events physically tired but emotionally rejuvenated.

It's intoxicating and the more you meet other authors, the more you crave the rush. That's why many return to the same events year after year.

MENTORS

Another great benefit to networking, online and offline, is the amount you can learn – and not just practical knowledge. Sure, there is a lot of that to be absorbed when distributors, agents, publishers, designers and authors are gathered in one place. Besides that, though, there's a mindset to learn.

There's a reason why some authors struggle to release a single novel per year while others chalk up 40. Not kidding. Some do that. Similarly, there's a reason why some authors only pull in a handful of sales per book launch while others consistently hit the *New York Times* bestsellers list with multiple pen names. In both cases, the two authors' ability levels, connections and knowledge might be similar. They both have the same 24 hours in a day. The only differences are how they think and act.

Do you have ability but lack the motivation? No problem. Hang around with positive, productive, successful role models long enough and you start to adopt their mindset. They don't even need to say anything; their actions set the bar and show you exactly what you need to do. Any insights they give are a bonus. In their presence, you can't help but improve your own habits and effort when you know how hard others work for better results.

The knowledge and wisdom of mentors like Mark Dawson, Rachel Abbott and Joanna Penn have benefited me greatly over the years. Just being with them at conferences and asking questions has yielded considerable value. Possibly without knowing it, they've helped me tighten my editing process, develop more effective marketing plans and quadruple the amount of words I write every year.

THE HIVE MIND

Another benefit of networking, particularly online, is the access it gives you to group knowledge. Wondering which version of a book cover is more likely to sell? Running a poll in a Facebook group of authors already killing it in that genre could be the answer. Need to know the best service that distributes your ebooks to different online bookstores? You can find a nuanced debate on the pros and cons of the major players. All you have to do is ask.

I tap into the hive mind all the time for anything from cover design to editing advice. In 2013, I wanted to feature lyrics from a famous Christmas song in one of my books. It was old and the original creator had died. However, I still wasn't sure if using the lyrics would breach copyright laws because – though I was only referencing a few lines – a music studio still held the rights.

Not knowing who to contact, or if I needed to contact anyone for permission at all, I took to Twitter. It didn't take long to receive replies. Authors I knew debated in the comments. When none could come to a concrete conclusion, one of them tagged in another writer they knew who had previously tackled the same issue – Scottish crime author Ian Rankin. He responded, stating that I did need permission because the quote I wanted to use ran over more than two lines. Another contributor also added details about who I would need to contact.

That's only one example of how the hive mind works. If you don't know something, the chances are someone you've met, or someone they know, will have the answer.

INDUSTRY SECRETS

In publishing, the landscape changes too fast for some publishers to keep up. Distributors go into liquidation. Online stores test new ads, unannounced. Mastermind groups covertly set up publishing houses with game-changing tactics. While inconvenient for most, changes like this provide a lucrative edge for in-the-know writers. And the benefits multiply if you're in a position to capitalise on what you learn ahead of the curve.

For example, back in 2017, major publisher *Macmillan* shut down *Pronoun*, which it had bought the previous year. At the time, *Pronoun* was a rising star in the publishing world. As a small tech company, it distributed ebooks for indie authors to multiple platforms that couldn't be reached through any other channel outside of traditional publishing – the main one being Google Books. Better yet, it did this without taking *any* royalty share from authors. It seemed too good to be true... and it was.

Noticing how quickly it was gaining market share, *Macmillan* bought *Pronoun* to secure its future. However, someone in the company must have realised quickly that *Pronoun*'s business model was unsustainable. Like many tech start-ups, it was banking on rapid growth to offset a lack of profitability. Unable to turn things around, *Macmillan* pulled the plug.

Well-connected authors who learned about the issue before it went public were able to work with *Pronoun*'s customer support team and get their titles moved to another distributor before the masses caused a backlog. That way, they avoided a sales blip while everyone else floundered.

Likewise, if you are aware of a new advertising platform with plenty of notice, you can learn how to optimise it before everyone else floods in and drives up the cost.

Recently, I got word of this exact scenario while chatting to an author friend over drinks. She told me that a well-known bookseller was trialling a new advertising platform. Not wanting to do so publicly, the company's executives invited a select group of highly successful authors to meet for a demonstration and she knew several of the attendees. Guess what they had in common? They had all attended the same event with the executive overseeing the operation. That one meeting gave them a significant advantage when it came to planning their next marketing manoeuvres.

Even if you're not invited to such a meeting, knowing about it can give you a significant advantage. I didn't have advance access to the portal, but I knew a change was coming and prepared ad copy ready for its launch. That's a huge advantage in itself!

As you become better connected, you find these industry secrets crop up more frequently. If you do a good enough job growing and strengthening your network, you could even find yourself in that early-access group.

The Help of Strangers

One of the best arguments in favour of networking follows the logic "you don't know *what* you don't know." Only it's more like, "you don't know *who* you *do* know." Ever run into a problem and thought, "if only I knew an investing expert"? Or a bodybuilder. Or a talk show host. You've likely done this. You've never met the person you have in mind and you know they are unlikely to help if you contact them directly.

Networking can come in handy here. Just because you don't know Oprah, The Rock or Stephen Fry, that doesn't mean you don't know someone who does. Or at the very least, they might know their agent.

Networking opens doors by getting you recommended as someone worth talking to. Think about it this way; if you're a powerful person and a stranger approaches you with a project, you'd be unlikely to consider it. But what if a friend you trust approaches you and introduces them: "Hey, this is my buddy. He knows what he's doing in the publishing world. Could he ask you a few questions?" In moments, the stranger has bypassed the obstacle of the stranger-danger filter. You're a friend of a friend. Plus, you "know what you're doing" so talking to you isn't a waste of time.

This is exactly what happened to me when I heard that Adam Croft, a bestselling thriller author whose latest book had briefly landed him above J K Rowling in the charts, was attending the same party as me in 2016. While sharing my enthusiasm with the event organiser, Orna Ross from the Alliance of Independent Authors, she cut me off.

"I know him! Let me introduce you," she said.

From that chance introduction, not only have we hung out several times at events, but I have also contacted him for publishing advice when I've run up against challenges that I know he has already overcome.

In some cases, this networking benefit can even save you time and money chasing red herrings. For example, you might think you really need to contact a certain celebrity to achieve a goal. You might discover, though, upon talking to someone in your network that the person you wished you knew has no decision-making power in that area. However, the *real* decision maker is a friend of a friend.

In these encounters with in-demand influencers, the right mutual friend can help you bypass having to reach fame to get their attention. All it takes is a simple character recommendation.

BUILD A SOCIAL KARMA BANK ACCOUNT

In goldmining, miners prospect by digging lots of holes until they find one that contains gold. Networking is similar but instead of digging dozens of holes, you help lots of people. You don't expect them all to come through for you – not every endeavour yields gold – but, inevitably, some will return the favour. The few that do will be worth the effort.

What this means is that you can count on your friends in times of need.

Sales a little low this month? Someone in your network could gush about your books to their fans because you did it for them a month ago.

Hired an editor one time when their biggest client left? Now that your regular editor is too busy to complete your project on time, they might allow you to jump to the front of their queue.

You're never sure exactly when your social karma bank account will pay out. The only certainty is the more deposits you make, the more you can count on getting a good return.

Gain Free Marketing Opportunities

If you know diddly squat about marketing, start by collecting your readers' email addresses because most successful creatives agree that having an active mailing list is one of the most powerful ways to grow a creative business.

Aside from enabling you to notify your readers when you have a launch, it also allows you to partake in a networking ecosystem that thrives on "newsletter swaps" – an activity in which authors endorse and promote each other's books (if they like them) during promotional periods. They do this by writing a quick review or mentioning that it's free or discounted in their own newsletter, not by giving their list to another author (because sharing readers' details is illegal, at least if you're dealing with European readers, not to mention immoral).

While this sounds more like marketing than networking advice, it straddles both topics. Authors value the mailing lists of other authors. If you have a large, responsive list, you can get onto the radar of prominent authors. The more powerful your list, the more authors will gravitate to you in the hope of gaining some reciprocal love.

It costs money to keep a mailing list but doing so gets you access to your peers' fans, usually for free. Plus, when you've appeared in each other's newsletters, it adds an extra layer of familiarity if you ever meet in real life.

Become a Speaker

Royalties from book sales are not the only source of income for many entrepreneurial authors. Some of the savviest also sell online courses and merchandise. However, one of the simplest ways to supplement your income is to speak, and networking can help you. Speaking requires no infrastructure, maintenance or overheads. Aside from the time it takes to prepare, the only costs you incur while speaking is your travel and living expenses, which are usually covered by your speaker's fee.

Speaking is built on relationships and reputation. Know someone who is running a book festival or writers' conference? Ask them to give you a stage from which to speak and you can start building a portfolio of experience. As long as you can get your expenses covered for the first few talks, you can afford to talk for free. That's because speakers sell books – often more than those who don't speak – and you can use these sales to supplement your speaker fee while you're getting started.

There's also the added benefit that speaking is a self-fuelling activity. Speak once and it'll earn you a fee and some book sales, plus new fans. Many of those fans will then recommend you to other event organisers where you can speak for larger sums and to bigger audiences.

While you might start by talking at literary events, many authors branch out to corporate and business networking events. That way, they can charge higher speaking fees. Prominent authors like J A Konrath, Mark Dawson and Seth Godin all report charging four or five figures for a single presentation.

It Creates a Virtuous Circle

Networking works as a virtuous circle: the more powerful connections you make, the more opportunities you receive, and the more opportunities you take, the more you make connections.

As a relatively unknown author, taking those early baby steps can seem daunting and/or fruitless. Perhaps that author you met at a local café could be just as clueless as you. Who do they know? Probably nobody right now but that doesn't mean it'll stay that way forever.

And that online group you joined? They use a ton of publishing jargon and you hate having to ask them to explain. Will that really help? Well, yes. If you're learning, you're growing. Knowing the jargon will help you hold your own in future conversations.

What you'll find over time is that networking gets easier. Experience makes it easier to approach people, partly because you get used to it and partly because they eventually hear about your reputation before they hear from you directly. Just because your first few attempts don't seem to make a difference, that doesn't mean it will be that way forever.

Quick Takeaways

The benefits of networking include:

- ✓ Understanding how different people achieve success
- ✓ Gaining genuine friends who share your passion
- ✓ Talking to mentors who can provide tailored advice
- ✓ Having access to a hive mind of knowledge and wisdom
- ✓ Hearing about industry changes ahead of the curve
- ✓ Receiving unforeseeable opportunities from strangers
- ✓ Bypassing social obstacles through referrals
- ✓ Building a social karma bank account
- ✓ Free marketing opportunities, like newsletter swaps
- ✓ Attracting paid speaking opportunities
- ✓ Forming a virtuous circle that compounds over time

3

YOUR NETWORKING DREAM TEAM

Your ideal network will comprise of individuals that can help you run a successful author business. In this section, I will provide a full list of the roles you will want to fill whether you are following a traditional or independent publishing path. If you want to pursue a traditional publishing career, publishers and agents fulfil much of these roles, or work with people who do. However, it is useful to understand every role in the team required to make an author a success regardless of your path because, as you grow, you might want to hire extra help to fill in the gaps not plugged by your publisher.

You don't have to hire all of these people full-time. That would be bad advice because many are only needed once in a while. The idea is simply to know at least one person in each of the following roles and hire them on a freelance basis when you need them. Done well, it will enable you to run a slick operation to rival the biggest publishers on the planet.

Editors

Without a doubt, an editor should be the first person you bring into your network. Good editors are priceless. Even authors who want to pursue traditional publishing sometimes hire editors to make their manuscript the best it can be *before* sending it an agent or publisher because it improves their chance of publication. For indies, editors are a must.

They can specialise in genres. Some are better at fantasy whereas others might work primarily on romance or thrillers. A non-fiction work on politics or business might need a politically minded editor to check tone. In contrast, a work of historical fiction might require an editor who specialises in that area to check dates and accuracy.

Mainly, though, no matter the genre, there are two types: developmental editors (who tackle plot holes, story structure, character development, etc.) and copy editors (who work on syntax and typos). Some authors like to work with a developmental editor first, clean up their manuscript, and then send it to another who specialises in copy editing. However, that's not always the case. The editors I've worked with can typically do both.

The main thing is to know a few. That way, if one is too busy, you can always work with another to get your latest project ready on time.

Cover Designers

Again, consider this a must. You typically won't need to fill this role if you have a publisher because they will usually have an in-house designer. However, I do know of an author who put his publisher in contact with a designer for his book covers, so it isn't always the case.

I have worked with three designers and while it can be tempting to do this work yourself if you're handy with Photoshop (as I once did and now regret), it isn't recommended. Book designers are specialists. They know your market, they understand what sells and they are able to meet reader expectations.

The truth is, readers do judge a book by its cover, and the right cover can multiply your sales tenfold. So, it's best to work with an expert.

Proofreaders

Proofreaders are your last line of defence against bad reviews. While you might not be published yet, and therefore might not have considered reviews, it is worth noting early. Make no mistake, if your work contains typos, readers will slash stars off it when they review it on retailer websites. As a result, this can have an impact on your sales and can decimate a launch.

One early bad review can put off new readers who aren't yet familiar with your work. Likewise, a manuscript infested with typos is unlikely to be considered by a publisher. Proofreaders aren't perfect – mistakes *always* slip through – but they are essential if you want to be considered professional.

Other Writers

The writers' lifestyle is a lonely one if you decide to work alone. For screenwriters, the dynamic is different because they have writers' rooms and are far more collaborative in their approach.

However, novelists tend to be lone wolves. As much as you might value your alone time, everybody struggles with too much of it.

The benefits of meeting other authors are plentiful and multifaceted. Not only do they provide knowledge and collaboration opportunities, but also moral support and a sense of community. I love my author friends. They understand my lifestyle, my struggles, and my reason for doing all of this, more so than my non-writing friends and family. Having them around has definitely improved my life.

PUBLISHERS

Publishers are good contacts because there are only so many hours in a day and not everybody wants to do everything themselves. If you're an entrepreneur at heart, then you can do a lot of the production, distribution and marketing yourself. However, not everybody is the same.

Even if you think you have everything under control, you can't reach everywhere. While you might have online sales nailed, you might struggle to get your books into airports and train stations. In that case, striking a deal with a publisher can truly benefit your business and help you to reach more readers.

If you're an independent author, it's good to know at least one publisher, if only to get some perspective on what opportunities lie on the opposite side of the fence. For those working with traditional publishers, or hybrid authors who self-publish some projects and work with publishers for others, knowing several publishers is the best practice. That way, if one doesn't like your current work in progress, you can always shop around with other commissioning editors who might love it.

Formatters/Typesetters

This role is often overlooked but is crucial, particularly if you publish independently. As a writer, the quality of your story and editing can determine the success of your books but so too can the layout. Pretty books sell better and provide a more satisfying reader experience.

This goes for print *and* ebook formats. If you don't know how to format both, it's worth knowing a formatter. Their work can turn a messy manuscript, full of uneven lines, into a polished book, complete with text-wrapped images and drop capitals. It's a specialty that really can help you stand out in a crowded marketplace of do-it-yourself publishers.

Distributors

This role encompasses traditional distributors like Gardners, Bertram Books or Ingram, as well as online retail distributors and booksellers like PublishDrive and Draft2Digital. These are the people who take your books and make them widely available to retailers and, sometimes, the public.

While it might seem that there's only so much these companies can do, not every book in their catalogues get the same level of attention. Therefore, getting to know the various distributors provides extra opportunities. For example, make a good impression on Draft2Digital's reps and it could lead to your book being recommended as an exciting new release to some of the internet's biggest retailers like Apple Books or Barnes & Noble. Kinga Jentetics at PublishDrive, on the other hand, has strong links to Chinese retailer Dangdang and the leading German ebook seller, Tolino.

These people can usually be found at major book fairs around the world, often manning a colourful stand. They can literally make you a star author in places and bookstores you might never have considered on your own.

AUDIOBOOK PRODUCERS

This one's a little more advanced but it's becoming more commonplace as audiobooks have made a resurgence into the mainstream. Audiobook producers come in many forms. Some are only producers and will help you adapt your book for a flat fee, running everything from casting voice actors to hiring sound engineers. Others are voice actors but can also produce your work, doing all of the required jobs needed to bring your book to market, again, for a one-off fee. Some will act and produce, but will accept a royalty share after the book is released instead of upfront payment. Their working practices vary a lot but all are equally valid. What your relationship with them looks like really depends on your goals.

I use a private production company called In Ear Entertainment. By delegating all of my audiobook production to the owner, Mark Chatterley, I have been able to save time by tapping into In Ear's existing bank of contacts. This move fast-tracked my ability to reach professional voice actors and sound experts and allowed me to focus my attention on building my network elsewhere that better suited my strengths. In my case, this setup has worked out well.

For others, however, a more hands-on approach can be the best strategy. While I learned about In Ear from another author, many writers wanting to adapt their book into audio find their producers on collaboration sites like Findaway Voices or Amazon's ACX. On ACX, you can send out your work and get auditions from voice actors who also double as their own producers. After you've chosen one you like, you can either choose to pay them upfront and get all future royalties yourself, or you can work together without exchanging money and both parties get a share of the audiobook's royalties once it starts selling.

WEB DESIGNERS

Your author website is your home on the internet and the one place you can control (unlike social media or retailers). For that reason, getting acquainted with a talented web designer can make all the difference to your business. A knowledgeable one will bring a boatload of value to your operation, enabling you to grow a mailing list, create an attractive blog, and stay up-to-date, optimising your site for mobile devices and new innovations.

While you can build your own website using services like Squarespace or Wix, it's still worth knowing a web designer. If you run into trouble, unable to untangle a piece of computer code or adapt your website in some way, that's when their expertise really sets your site apart from the amateurs.

MARKETING CONSULTANTS

This person is only necessary if you have a business focus and want to turn your writing into a career. I have taken courses delivered by marketing consultants and like to ask them questions regularly on social media. That way, I can stay on top of trends and maximise my book sales for the lowest possible cost.

If you're doing very well, you can hire one for one-to-one training. Although, while it might be tempting to outsource your marketing to a service provider or consultant, it's always best to run this part of your business yourself if you can. Talking to multiple marketers can give you an all-round knowledge and nobody will care as much as you when it comes to saving wasted money.

PUBLICISTS

Again, a more advanced team player, publicists are people who focus on free advertising as opposed to the paid options explored by traditional marketers. Typically, their functions include talking to journalists to get you exposure in magazines or on the radio and TV. They can even get you book signings and speaking gigs at coveted venues.

Many proactive, traditional authors work with publicists hired inhouse by their publisher. Yet, they also choose to work with a private publicist who will work specifically on their books.

It's possible to do this sort of work yourself. However, it's worth getting to know those who know what they're doing. A good publicist has connections that might have taken years to build. They also know how to write an amazing pitch that cuts through the noise received by journalists, which they can teach you.

TRANSLATORS

As their readership grows, many authors discover a demand for their books in other languages. However, producing that work in a language you don't speak personally is impossible without help. Free translation software such as Google Translate is improving all the time but it isn't a reliable translator beyond the scope of individual words. That's why it's useful to add translators to your networking dream team. They can help you produce a book translation or check the quality of a translation that has been produced by a third party on your behalf. Not only that, they can also help you to come up with marketing materials like newsletters and paid adverts.

You can find good translators at your local university or on websites that match paying clients with freelancers, such as Fiverr or PeoplePerHour. However, if you want to pursue this route, it's always important to check the quality of any translation you receive with a second translator until you've established a trusted relationship. Even then, you will need one to proofread the other's work if you want to look professional. You don't just want someone who can speak and write in your chosen language; you want someone who can write and edit to a professional standard.

Street Team Members

Getting people to review your books and spread the word can be difficult, particularly as a new writer. The solution to this problem is to build a street team – also known as a launch team, review team or advanced reader team. This is a simple concept: in essence, your street team is a group of your most avid readers.

When you start, your team can be made up of reliable friends and family members who read in your genre. But, as your career develops, you can ask your true readers to join. The parameters of your relationship is easily defined: you give them your new books for free in ebook form via email before their official release dates. In response, they agree to write a review online to help you build up some social proof, ready to sell to new readers in the weeks or months following your launch.

Agents

Agents are negotiators. They can get you a deal or improve one you've already managed to get on your own. You have to give them a cut of the profit for this effort (usually 15-20%) but the difference they can make to you career can be life-changing because they can get you through doors you won't be able to open alone.

For example, there are lots of large publishers who simply won't work with authors that don't have an agent. They don't accept unsolicited manuscripts (those not approved by an agent) so it's the only way to reach them. Film and TV works in a similar way.

If you're an indie you might want to handle your own book publishing process in English (or your native language) but agents are able to broker translation deals, movie deals, and merchandise deals. A good agent is your best ambassador and an expert who knows how to dissect a contract to protect you from giving away too many intellectual property rights.

LAWYERS

Lawyers come in many forms: corporate, housing, family, criminal, intellectual property, etc. Not all lawyers know all laws. They specialise. Typically, the only ones you are likely to need on your networking dream team are an intellectual property lawyer and a contract lawyer. This is because, like agents, they can protect you from a bad contract. Unlike agents, however, they don't have a vested interest in the particulars of the contract so they can work completely unbiased.

Having them around can protect you from a bad agent's contract. However, they also have other uses. For a start, if you write non-fiction, they can help you to avoid getting sued if you plan on using the names of real people. The chances are, you won't need a lawyer when you first start publishing, but they become a necessity as you grow and gain the attention of opportunists looking to syphon away your hard-earned success.

ACCOUNTANTS

Publishing is a business, and whether you're an indie author or you get your royalties from a publisher, you'll need to file a tax return no matter how large or small your royalties might be. In each case, knowing a good accountant can greatly improve the amount of money you keep.

I know lots of authors who value their accountant as one of their best contacts. As savvy businesspeople, they rave about all the *legal* ways their accountant has saved them money. Whether that is teaching them to incorporate their business or advising them on which expenses of their professional life can be claimed to offset their tax liability. If you want to be professional, it's worth having one on your team.

TRADE ORGANISATIONS

Organisations such as the Alliance of Independent Authors (ALLi) and the Society of Authors (SoA) are groups of professionals that help authors to fill in the gaps that are missing from their dream team. If you need help with something, these are the places to go. They will help you with contracts, provide marketing advice and put you in touch with relevant people if nobody is on hand to help you with a specific query. Depending on the organisation, some provide watchdog services to test whether other organisations and services can be trusted. You have to pay to be a member but some services are free and available to non-members.

The key here is to look at this list and work out which roles you need to fill in your dream team. Not every author's team will look the same. While some people might want every one of these roles filled, others might not need to work with half of them. Others, meanwhile, might have specialised needs and want extra roles filled that aren't even on this list. The choice is yours.

Quick Takeaways

Roles in your networking dream team might include:

- ✓ Accountants
- ✓ Agents
- ✓ Audiobook producers
- ✓ Authors
- ✓ Cover designers
- ✓ Distributors
- ✓ Editors
- ✓ Formatters
- ✓ Lawyers
- ✓ Marketing consultants
- ✓ Proofreaders
- ✓ Publicists
- ✓ Publishers
- ✓ Street team members
- ✓ Trade organisations
- ✓ Translators
- ✓ Web designers

4

Dealing with Shyness or Technophobia

By assembling your dream team, you can explore plenty of networking opportunities online and in the real world. How many you check out is up to you. Each comes with its own benefits. You don't have to try them all – just what aligns with your personality and goals.

Whatever you choose to focus on will probably depend on whether you identify as shy or extroverted, a technophobe or technophile. These factors will sway which networking options you enjoy – at first. However, that can change as your experiences and skillset grow.

The reason this section groups together technophobes and introverts is because, in networking, struggling in either one of these areas can cause the same problem: lacking a voice in a community that can provide you with opportunities.

Often, when people identify as a technophobe or being shy, they don't fully understand their potential. They believe they can't succeed in certain ways because of stories they have always told themselves – beliefs that they allow to limit their personal growth. As a result, they tailor their behaviour, creating a self-fulfilling prophecy where they never try anything that challenges their assumptions.

For example, lots of us have watched TV shows and movies in which stereotypical elderly characters express bewilderment at new technology. In doing so, they repeat the same mantras:

"Computers are hard."

"I'm getting too old for these new-fangled gadgets."

"Of course kids can use technology. They're born into it!"

Despite countless examples of elderly people working at the forefront of technological fields and using computers in their everyday lives, many adults stop adopting new technology when they hit a certain age. They internalise what they see on TV and see learning as a battle they will inevitably lose as they age. They believe this and perceive it as a universal truth.

Then they stop trying which only validates their beliefs. Once a limiting belief has taken hold, they close off their minds to new experiences, teaching themselves that what they believe is true, even if their opinions are based on biased experiences.

Unless they become self-aware.

When it comes to computing, learning the basics is possible and *will* help you network in the publishing industry, particularly if you're starting from scratch. You don't have to be a computer scientist. Just knowing how to get online and type short messages to new contacts will get you to where you want to be.

The same goes for shyness. Not everyone can – or wants to – deliver a compelling keynote speech at a corporate dinner. Attending a few events and chatting quietly with one like-minded creative at a time, however, is achievable. What's more, it really will make your presence known in the publishing community, which will be of benefit to your career and sense of belonging.

Overcoming shyness and technophobia is equally possible. All you have to do is take small steps, as you will soon see.

OVERCOMING TECHNOPHOBIA

Being a technophobe is no longer a barrier to using social media. Large platforms like Facebook and Pinterest are designed to be as user-friendly as possible. That's why over 3.48 billion people – nearly 45% of the world's population – have some form of social media presence, according to the leading social media scheduling app Hootsuite. Social media companies cater for the lowest common denominator: if you can turn on a computer, you can almost certainly run a social media account and answer emails.

Even if you have never turned on a computer, it's possible to learn. Technology companies design products so that children can use them intuitively, so much so that most devices no longer come with printed instruction manuals. Toddlers can often use tablets before they can speak or walk.

One major barrier a technophobe might encounter is the inability to type quickly. Tech companies have addressed that too. Thanks to voice-to-text software like *Dragon Naturally Speaking* by Nuance it's possible to dictate and watch your computer type your words out for you. Industry juggernauts like

Amazon and Google are nurturing a voice-first generation of children who view typing as a second option. In short, having limited technical ability need no longer be a barrier.

Using Shyness to Your Advantage

Being shy is a common reason why new writers don't step into the networking arena. It makes sense: the publishing community is abundant with quiet, bookish individuals who enjoy locking themselves away, living in worlds that exist entirely inside their heads. As writers, we are mostly a community of introverts, but that doesn't mean you can't act extroverted.

One reason why many people avoid physical networking events for the long term is that they misunderstand what it means to be introverted. It doesn't necessarily mean that you are destined to suffer paralysing shyness and awkward interactions. This can happen but it isn't inevitable. And being shy certainly isn't an all-encompassing disadvantage, particularly in rooms full of other introverts.

While energetic, extroverted individuals love bustling social groups, not everyone caught up in those circles necessarily feels the same way. Often, introverts seek opportunities to bond with one another, preferring one-to-one interactions with quieter conversation partners. Those with introverted personalities also seek to slow down conversations so they can digest information in detail and provide a more thoughtful response. Sometimes, that makes them *better* at forming deep connections.

Either way, nobody is purely introverted or extroverted. Nobody can stand to live alone for their entire life without talking to another human being. As much as they enjoy the *idea* of spending an evening in silence, curled up with a book, a month or more of solitude, in all likelihood, would send most people climbing the walls. Personalities are complex and most people exist on a shifting spectrum between shy and extroverted, impossible to pin into one specific character profile forever.

No matter whether you consider yourself a technophobe, a technophile, shy or extroverted, you don't have to let that label dictate your destiny. A skilled networker needs a variety of skills and you will have to practise them all. There is no limit to your ability – only what you are willing to try.

Quick Takeaways

If you struggle with shyness or technophobia:

- ✓ You don't have to nail every strategy to succeed
- ✓ Where you focus your energy will depend on your personality
- ✓ Computers are now intuitive so can be mastered easily
- ✓ Dictation software means that a slow typing speed is no longer an issue
- ✓ Shy people can also do well at real-world networking
- ✓ Nobody is a pure introvert or extrovert

NETWORKING
ONLINE

5

PLACES TO NETWORK ONLINE

When I started writing, I had no idea where to begin networking. Fortunately, the book trade has one of the most generous, inclusive groups of professionals in the world – particularly writers. They welcome total newbies and are often happy to show them the ropes. Once you find them, in many cases, the problem isn't getting them to talk – it's making them stop!

"But where do I find them?" I hear you ask.

Well, that's exactly what this chapter will explore. Due to the low cost and ease of access for most people, online is usually the best place to start.

Remember, you don't have to visit all of these places at once. The idea is to start small and challenge yourself more as your confidence, ability and network develops.

SOCIAL MEDIA

Social media is a great place to start, particularly as a novice. The reason is simple: it's easy to find role models and shadow their behaviour until you develop your own style.

An easy way to find the type of contacts you want is to search hashtags they are likely to use on Twitter or Instagram. A hashtag is a clickable message that groups content together on some social media websites. To create one, you type the hash symbol (#), followed by a short message, without spaces. All messages that contain the same hashtag lead users to a single feed that shows similar content in one place. Examples for writers include:

#WriteClub
#NaNoWriMo
#AmWriting

A quick Google search will give you other options. Once you've found influencers you like and seen how they're making connections, you can replicate their behaviour to reach out to other authors and build your reputation.

The crime and children's author Anthony Horowitz is an excellent case study for this topic. His tweets are a balanced stream of entertainment, inspiration and education – three key components of a strong social media presence. When he isn't giving his readers an insight into his writing process, he's sharing photos of his exploits, supporting charities, or reviewing books written by other authors. Occasionally, he will plug one of his books, but the majority of his messages are dedicated to providing value to others.

Some of my earliest author-friends came from Twitter and talked about the same things I did: book covers, hitting daily wordcount targets, awesome writing podcasts. You would be surprised who reaches out to you based on the things you write. Some users come across as a little salesy and disingenuous at first but ultimately that's because, like you, they're trying to work out how to network effectively and are making mistakes along the way.

Twitter, like Instagram, has limits because it favours celebrity culture and virality over personal connections.

Facebook, on the other hand, favours smaller groups. It's easier to be heard there, compared to Twitter's ocean of noise. You can have more intimate conversations with specific groups of people, set up collaborative projects and even wall off conversations to include only relevant users. The platform's trade-off for lacking the same virality as other platforms is providing its users with the ability to reach and stay in contact with the *right* people.

Reddit offers a hybrid scenario. As a microblogging platform, it allows users to submit questions and discuss subjects on pages broken up by topic. These "subreddits" are go-to places for writers of all kinds. They form communities of users with similar interests and rank well on Google so offer the potential for virality.

Goodreads is a site specifically for readers and those in the book business. Authors use it to network and promote each other's work. The audience is smaller than the more dominant social media sites but the book focus can pack a punch, particularly if you are active.

The same goes for Wattpad, a site for writers to post their stories as free instalments in exchange for reader comments. Many writers meet there and support each other by interacting with their stories and collaborating.

Each site's potential depends on your goals as a writer. If you plan to build a strong network of corporate clients so you can speak at their events, Linkedin will likely be your best option.

If you want to reach influencers in China then the best options would be WeChat or Sina Weibo.

It's worth weighing up the potential advantages and drawbacks of each platform before investing time in the wrong one.

EMAILS

Emails can be your best option if you aim to form a strong connection with the recipient of your words. I'm not talking about newsletters. That's marketing, not networking. I'm talking about old-fashioned one-to-one email conversations.

I regularly talk to authors, bloggers and distributors like modern-day pen pals. These conversations started that way for good reason: in each case we met at an event and continued the conversation via the other's website contact page. Or I edited their book, or we contributed to the same anthology.

In these cases, each conversation blossomed from a physical meeting or a shared project. However, it doesn't have to be that way. It's fine to fire up a conversation by asking a question over a blog post they wrote or to propose a collaborative project if you think you can deliver value.

There are no set rules, only etiquette. As long as you're not spamming, entering someone's email inbox separates you from the competition on social media and makes you more memorable. Indeed, if you follow this book's advice about adding value, your emails should evolve into a welcomed read for even the busiest of authors.

Blogs

Speaking of adding value, there are few better ways to help another writer than to create valuable content for their blog. I've reached out via email several times in this way and it has resulted in being on good terms with a number of bloggers.

The key to getting featured is being thorough. Before you approach anyone, first read their existing articles and take notes based on the length, structure, subject matter and style of each post. When you email, it's good to come up with a selection of ideas so they can pick a favourite. I usually pre-write and edit a draft of the one I think is best, but also give them backup options.

Remember, it's about appealing to *their* audience and adding value to *their* site, not flogging your stuff. Most bloggers will allow you to add a few self-promotion links at the end of your post anyway so, if you do a good job, people will check you out after reading the article. A pure sales pitch will be ignored.

The networking benefits are twofold. Not only do you put yourself onto an influential blogger's radar, but you also increase your reputation with their readers. I've been recognised at events a handful of times for a post I wrote for Jane Friedman's blog or for Mark Dawson's *The Self-Publishing Formula*.

If you run a blog of your own, you can interview influential writers for your site. An interview can cost them 30-60 minutes but that's a small price to pay for drumming up book sales. In return, you get to ask a potential mentor a series of your most pressing questions.

Podcasts

Podcasts are like online radio shows you can listen to, pause and skip through at your leisure. Typically, they have a talk-show format with a host and guest but sometimes they work more like a radio play with a narrator.

Initially run by amateurs in home studios, these productions have swelled in popularly and professionalism over the past decade. In its latest series, the biggest, *Serial*, boasted over five million downloads *per episode*. As networking options go, this is one of the most outgoing choices you can try online. However, this is one of the few ways you can make a connection without standing in front of a live audience. If the content is live-streamed (as it is with some podcasters) you can answer audience questions in real time.

Admittedly, if you appear as a guest on a podcast, you might have to dress up a little, as many podcasters also stream your webcam footage directly to YouTube, like live TV. Or they record it on Zoom and broadcast an edited version later. But who's to know if you're wearing shorts and bunny slippers below the waist?

Being new and inexperienced shouldn't hold you back, either, because it's often an angle that interests podcasters. Educational podcasts for authors are aimed primarily at newbies, so hosts occasionally interview newcomers to uncover their challenges.

An appearance can push you ahead of 99% of authors who won't step into the spotlight because they aren't comfortable being recorded. By ignoring that discomfort, you get to work in an environment that contains less competition from authors.

If that sounds good but, for whatever reason, you can't get on one, you could always start your own. Many authors will happily be a guest if someone else is running the show, even if the production is basic and the audience is small. In the long run, it would actually work out better for you than appearing elsewhere because it means getting to interview guests *you* want to meet and growing your own influence as a host.

QUICK TAKEAWAYS

When it comes to networking online:

- ✓ The author community welcomes newbies
- ✓ Join a few social media platforms to find your tribe
- ✓ Model your activity on influencers who have the type of presence you want
- ✓ Find communities by searching for hashtags and groups
- ✓ Use email to create more memorable bonds with individuals
- ✓ Write blog posts to reach out to influencers
- ✓ Appear on podcasts to fast-track your reputation as a recognisable face and voice

6

STARTING ONLINE RELATIONSHIPS

There are at least four million published authors on Earth, but your potential contact pool is actually much bigger. Besides professional novelists, there are scriptwriters, poets, journalists and well-connected unpublished hobbyists. Then there are all manner of designers, marketers and other creative specialists who can add value and help you grow your writing business. All good connections, many of these people can be found on social media and are more amenable to being contacted there than in the real world.

Sticking to writers, think of it this way: imagine you saw someone typing away in a coffee shop, extended your hand and said, "Hey. I'm a writer too. Wanna be friends?" How do you think they'd react? Chances are, they'd give you a funny look, shut down the conversation and use a different café. After all, you look like a crazy person.

They're wondering what you're talking about, interrupting them while they're finishing their overdue economics paper. A writer? Naw! They just have a man bun and like to work in a coffee shop because their roommates won't stop playing music.

You got the wrong guy.

Online is a different story. Many book trade professionals declare exactly who they are and what they like on their social media profile. This makes it easy to spot a good contact and gives you an ice-breaker. They are also far more likely to check out your profile and accept friend requests, bypassing the "are-you-crazy?" stage. In some cases, they seek you out first. You might be surprised who's watching your posts with interest.

For example, in early 2019, I visited a publishing event in London where, at a party, I recognised a man from *somewhere* online. I couldn't quite place him, but it quickly became obvious that he knew me when, at the bar, he said, "Dan! Nice to meet you. I recognised you from Facebook. I'm Darren."

"Oh yeah?" I asked, cradling a beer. "Thanks, Darren. Nice to meet you too. Which Facebook group? I'm in a lot."

"20Books," he said. "I've seen you answering questions on the posts. You're one of the more active members."

Darren Hassall, a Young Adult fantasy and thriller author. It clicked. We had spoken several times in the comments of Facebook posts. And there it was; an online ice-breaker I didn't know had happened, catapulting me to first-name terms with a proactive writer in a bar halfway across the country. Bear in mind that this connection came from a group containing more than 30,000 people!

I wasn't a group admin, nor did I establish it, yet I made an impression. Social media introductions work, and it's never too late to get involved.

CREATE A SOCIAL MEDIA ACCOUNT

Okay, we're starting *really* basic here but it's important to know *how* to set up an account tailored to networking.

Firstly, you don't need to be everywhere. Spreading yourself too thinly across multiple platforms will result in giving up before you gain any traction. Plenty of successful, well-connected authors limit themselves to one or two, in some cases, setting up profiles on others and simply writing a message to direct visitors to their active profiles.

At the time of writing this book, the most interesting platforms for writers are Facebook, Twitter, Instagram, Pinterest and Wattpad. Each functions differently and has different user demographics. Do some research to ensure you're entering the right community before you invest too much time. As mentioned in the section "Places to Network Online" each social media platform requires different skills to succeed and appeals to a different audience. Just because your readers hang out primarily on one platform, writers or booksellers might prefer to be somewhere else.

Pinterest, an image-sharing community, is known for appealing to women in their thirties. Therefore, it has a strong community of mothers. If you're a children's author, you may want a Pinterest presence to reach these mothers and influence them to buy your books for their children. However, you won't necessarily find other children's authors there to talk to about marketing. Their primary focus there will be to appeal to readers, not writers. If you want to meet them in a networking capacity, Facebook or Twitter are probably better options.

It's a good idea to vet sites for their networking potential but also for the skills required to succeed on them. Twitter favours short-form content and wit. Facebook favours long-form writing and video. Instagram and Pinterest require an ability to create beautiful images. Which of these you choose should depend on your skills and goals.

Once you've chosen, you'll want to craft your profile with the intention of showing you're a writer. That means creating banners containing your books (or at least a quote that indicates you're a writer if you're unpublished) and a personable, relevant personal description.

To attract the right sort of friends, you'll need to be explicit about your writing identity in your bio, images and any links you provide. Proofread carefully to eliminate typos and off-brand content to look professional. Essentially, this exercise is about letting potential contacts know you're worth their time.

Don't lie or exaggerate your achievements, but do present yourself as an attractive prospect who can deliver value. Once you've expressed exactly who you are and what you can do, you can start networking!

Don't Sell

If you take one lesson from this book, let it be that cold selling does not sell books. It alienates your social media friends before the conversation has even started. Trust me. I tried this tactic when I first started and had no clue how to network. Authors complain about it frequently. It's right up there alongside asking someone to like your Facebook page the moment they accept your friend request.

There are people who follow or friend anyone they think might vaguely be interested in their book and then – as soon as their request gets accepted – they send a pitch:

Hey!
I see you're a fantasy fan. So am I. I love it so much I even write it! Check out my book, *Fantasy Title*. You won't regret it!
www.link.com/fantasytitle

Short, sweet and painfully formulaic. There's no preamble, no relationship-building and no context. That's annoying enough if you're a reader. If you're a writer, it's cringeworthy. Many writers *do* read in their genre but their reading list is usually overloaded as it is.

Authors who do this mean well but have flawed logic, mainly because they have two competing goals. They want to have a friendly relationship with the recipient *and* sell them books. By comparison, do builders network with other construction workers by trying to sell them a house renovation? No. They share ideas and funny anecdotes in the hope of eventually getting a referral.

Your best bet for making friends is to help them and form a bond over common interests. Be a person, not a salesman.

ACT LIKE A NATIVE

Typical users don't have an agenda on social media. They don't sell. They act like humans. However, *how* humans act depends on where you are. In the real world, culture influences human behaviour and it's the same online.

Just because you know the social etiquette on one site, that doesn't mean the same strategy will work on another. For example, if you posted lengthy humorous stories on Instagram (as you would on Facebook) your content would never gain traction. Instagram natives want striking images that can be consumed at a glance. If text is included, it's typically only a phrase Photoshopped onto a picture.

Pre-scheduled, automated content, pumped to multiple platforms, is easy to spot. If someone includes a string of hashtags in a Facebook post, most people know that content was probably piped from Twitter or Instagram. Thus, they also know that any comments on the post will be ignored because the poster is focused on another platform. As a result, many users never bother interacting.

To avoid these *faux pas* yourself, model your behaviour on successful native users until you're comfortable enough to establish your own style. Using each platform authentically, while adding value to other users in the ways they prefer, is a sure-fire way to create a good impression.

Find Your Community

Many niche publishing communities exist on each platform, each with different purposes. One way to find them is to follow relevant hashtags on Twitter and Instagram (e.g. #AuthorsOfInstagram, #AmWriting) that group together like-minded people. Alternatively, you could join Facebook groups explicitly set up for writers (e.g. 20BooksTo50K, SPF Community, The Indie Author Mindset).

Pro Tip: when you join a group, read its rules *before* posting to avoid angering the admins. They're usually pinned at the top of the page and each group works differently.

It's a good idea to start with writers' groups because you'll immediately have something in common. However, you should be aware that other groups exist – for designers, publicists, booksellers, etc. – and it is in your interests to establish a presence with them too.

For example, you could join cover design groups where authors and cover designers critique each other's work. Designers ask authors who are selling well to share what elements of their covers appeal to particular readers, and authors post early drafts they have been sent by designers to get group feedback. These exchanges lead to better covers all round but also keep the community alive.

Similar groups exist for distributors, dictation enthusiasts, audiobook creators and event organisers. Plus, there are techie groups where members help each other correct issues with their websites or online ads. How many groups you want to contribute to depends on how diverse you want your network to be. And, if you discover a niche that isn't being covered, you could always start one yourself.

ASK VALUABLE QUESTIONS

Think you can't add value to a large group of experts? Well, you need to give yourself more credit. As a group matures, it develops its own jargon and acronyms known only to experienced members. Their discussions develop too, moving away from the basics to more advanced themes. Some groups have a "hall of fame" section where users can see information on the fundamentals. However, this isn't always the case.

As a newbie, you can add real value and get yourself noticed by asking great questions. For example, I mentioned the issue of jargon and acronyms. D2D, PD, AMS, Going Wide, BookBub ads — these are all terms that experienced indie authors will know but newbies couldn't possibly guess. You could search each of them one-by-one but asking the question benefits both you and the group. For example:

> "Guys, I need an indie author jargon dictionary. Could you comment with a well-known publishing term or acronym and then put the definition next to it?"

This post in itself doesn't add value to the established members who already know what each term means. However, it will help newer authors coming in behind you. As site admins can point to it as an FAQ resource for new members, they will appreciate your contribution. Just check it hasn't already been done.

If you're trying to network but fear you have nothing to contribute to the discussion, you needn't worry: your newness can be an asset.

RESEARCH YOUR MENTORS

Once you've asked questions and established yourself as an active community member, you'll want to identify your best mentors. Who is most knowledgeable and generous with their time? It should be easy to spot them by the tell-tale markers of their success in their comments: "I've written 20 books and discovered…"; "You should do this. It quadrupled my income and…"

These people are success stories for a reason. They know their subject and are willing to help others. The fact that they're generous with their time is a bonus and the reason you'll want them in your network.

Knowing who's who and what they do is key in networking circles. Even if you're not close enough to call them friends (yet), knowing what they know means you can connect them with other people with similar interests. Once that mentor figure sees you making connections on their behalf, they are far more likely to check out your work and see you as a peer.

ADD FRIENDS AND BECOME A CHEERLEADER

Do you know the active players in your genre(s)? Great! Now is the time to follow them or send friend requests. Remember, you're not trying to sell anything to them. Your primary objective is to ensure that these people know you, like you and come to trust you.

The path to achieving this goal is straightforward: be a role model, keep on their radar by commenting on their posts (not in a sycophantic way) and add value where you can. Also, recommend their books *if* you believe they're good. Be a genuinely interested and interesting person. Stick to these methods and you can't go far wrong.

These people aren't your rivals. In the publishing industry, despite the charts and league tables, your contemporaries are far more like colleagues than enemies. The best way to get ahead is not to cut throats and burn bridges. It's to collaborate, share knowledge and be a cheerleader; encourage others when they're down and congratulate them when they're ahead.

Join Paid Clubs and Take Courses

If you're short of time and want to fast-track your networking, you can enrol in courses or join clubs. Typically, these clubs are professional organisations that require a subscription fee. Examples of professional organisations include the Alliance of Independent Authors (ALLi), Society of Authors (SoA), and Independent Publishers' Guild (IPG). There are many others. These communities cost money to enter but offer extensive resources in return. Plus, they provide networking opportunities for members, sometimes in Facebook groups, other times at events.

Courses work in much the same way. Lots of successful author-entrepreneurs run online courses which you can take. Many also have communities associated with the courses. These often come in two tiers of access – one for potential students and another for paying members.

Accessing the paid-only tier can be invaluable. Not only do you get a great course mentor but you also get help from long-term "graduate" students who help new starters to interpret and implement the information. Groups also save you time by separating the serious professionals willing to invest in their development from hobbyists. This separation allows you to focus on more promising contacts from day one.

Of course, don't pay for courses if you don't have the money. Paying can save you a lot of time but not all courses are created equal, and free options can work equally well.

ADD VALUE

It doesn't take long to work out the big names in any online group. Everyone knows who they are because they're extremely active and their comments are packed with valuable information. Examples include Adam Croft, Joanna Penn and Michael Anderle. These are people who walk the walk, nail their author strategy and share *a lot* of what they learn along the way, despite potentially giving up their competitive edge as a result.

Once you've established your presence it's good to answer questions, ask questions and share information that the group will find useful. Had a great launch? Tell the gang exactly what you did to shift 1,000 copies. Made a mistake that ruined your launch? Share that too! That way, others will avoid the same pitfall and appreciate the heads-up. The key is to bypass your pride and add value.

If you have a quiet month then say how much you appreciate others' contributions. Cheerleaders are needed to boost morale as much as powerhouses are needed to pave the path to success.

ACTIONS TO TAKE

To start networking online, you should:

- ✓ Create a social media account
- ✓ Use groups or hashtags to find your desired community
- ✓ Participate in public online groups to attract *relevant* connections
- ✓ Act like a native on each platform
- ✓ Expect contact from fellow writers
- ✓ Optimise your social media profiles to show potential contacts your interests and worth
- ✓ Never start conversations with a sales pitch
- ✓ Ask valuable questions until you can contribute knowledge to group discussions
- ✓ Research those who answer your questions as these mentors often make great contacts
- ✓ Celebrate others' success because teamwork gets you further than competition
- ✓ Join organisations, associations or clubs, or take courses to save time filtering connections
- ✓ Share your secrets to provide as much value as possible

7

STRENGTHENING ONLINE RELATIONSHIPS

A strong show of initial effort should get you accepted into the online publishing community. Then what? Well, Rome wasn't built in a day and neither is a reputation. Just because you're known, that doesn't mean you're respected. Notice how I've only mentioned a handful of names in this book and most are super-successful self-published authors? That's because they tick those boxes for me. I know them. I respect them. They've been prominent for a while. I'm interested in any project that has their name attached.

That's rare. Many authors gain networking success but only for a short time. They gather lots of friends and followers as their star rises. However, they struggle to maintain their position at the top.

Generally, these shooting stars fall into two camps.

Some allow their light to go dark when they become successful enough because they can afford it. They take their foot off the throttle and live "the good life" with their business ticking over in the background.

Others who fall away tend to be those who never *loved* the industry in the first place. They climbed the social hierarchy because they saw its potential but didn't work with sustained passion. After a while, they got bored and moved on to new challenges outside publishing.

Then there is a third group who persist. The type who become big names through relentless enthusiasm. They seem to be everywhere, connected to everyone, all while ploughing forward with a successful author career: Amanda M. Lee, Michael Anderle, Mark Dawson and Joanna Penn are names that spring to mind. Each make a six- or seven-figure income every year and are regular contributors in the author networking scene.

That's the person you might want to become – a permanent fixture in the cosmos, not some burned-up shooting star. This next section focuses on creating longevity as a connected author using online methods.

BE CONSISTENT

At one end, publishing is a revolving door of beginners. Some stay while most vanish into the fog after a disappointing initial book launch. At its other extreme, publishing is a cliff where aged veterans race toward oblivion. People give up, people retire, people die but new faces appear all the time. That's why maintaining a consistent presence is so important. It means you keep filling your network with new people to balance out those who have left.

Taking a break means you risk popping up after a year and finding that your friends have disappeared. And if that happens, you have no choice but to start over. Being a good writer and a savvy entrepreneur won't matter to potential collaborators if no one can vouch for your reputation.

Consistency helps you to avoid this frustrating scenario. It means that you always have *someone* to sing your praises to new starters as they enter the industry. It also means that you never disappoint your network, which is important in an industry where the contributors that survive are usually the ones that consistently meet their audience's expectations.

A few years ago, being consistent as an influencer meant putting out content regularly. A video, a newsletter, a book – it didn't matter. What mattered was quality and regularity, whether those principles were applied to releasing a new book every year or a newsletter on the same day every month.

Website algorithms (the code that dictates how sites function) have accelerated this requirement. They've done this by burying content by inconsistent performers and promoting the work of producers with a reliable track record. Basically, websites benefit most from their most popular content producers, so they give those producers extra exposure.

YouTubers talk about this phenomenon frequently in their videos: release a video on the same day every week and your audience grows to expect it. Every seventh day, people show up at your channel looking for your latest instalment. It skyrockets your popularity.

Miss a week and people start to lose faith in you. They might return the next week but too many gaps and they'll stop looking and will find another creator. Or they'll stop watching YouTube altogether, simply because you weren't consistent.

Those in charge want to retain users, so they create algorithms that reward prolific creators regardless of whether their videos require less time and effort to create.

Ecommerce sites do the same thing, favouring books by authors who constantly have something new to offer over those who haven't published in years. Likewise, Facebook and Twitter analyse which posts and users are popular so they can serve the best content to users. This, in turn, keeps them scrolling for longer.

When you first start out, even in a group, you'll find that getting seen is like swimming upstream. However, once you've built a good reputation, the network's algorithms gradually give your posts more exposure, favouring yours over those of other users.

It's a win-win, as long as you've got a strong history with the algorithms. But you have to keep feeding the beast. Take a break and you risk falling out of favour and having to start from scratch.

The lesson here? Be consistent. Your readers want consistent book releases, website algorithms want consistent content, and your network needs consistent input to stay aware of how much value you provide.

Be Professional

Lapses happen all the time on social media. People get frustrated and jealousy takes over. It's easy to understand why, when everyone's work is public and some individuals see overnight success while others struggle for years. We all have bad moments when we let our guard slip and throw a tantrum. For most people, this isn't an issue. There are no consequences.

But that's not the case for creative professionals whose livelihoods rely on their reputations.

Public celebrity meltdowns often make the news. Not only does this damage their reputation with their fans but it also makes them seem like a loose cannon – potentially hazardous to any project.

Knowing how to act professionally on social media is simple if you think of it like delivering a speech. Most public figures wouldn't step on stage and rant about someone in the room. Yet many do it on social media, forgetting that they're followed by thousands or even millions of people.

That's not to say you can't have a bad day. Just consider editing your rage into something constructive *before* you hit send. Instead of ranting, swearing and name-calling, try:

Ugh. This author stuff is a slog today, guys. I write every day, release three titles a year and advertise my work but I still can't see any progress. If it doesn't turn around soon, I'm giving up. Everyone else seems to be nailing it around me and I can't understand what I'm missing. Any ideas?

Firstly, notice there's no swearing? Some authors *can* hit their network with obscene rants, but few are able to pull it off and walk away unscathed. Using a constructive method like this yields more benefits. On occasions where authors have cried for help, I've seen editors, designers and marketers all jump in to work out where they're going wrong.

The key is to respond with integrity if this happens to you. After all, they have gone out of their way to help fix your bad day. What they say might not be what you want to hear, and it may mean taking on extra work, but it will be of benefit to you.

Don't hit back or get defensive if you want to become well-connected and keep your connections. It's unprofessional, not to mention emotionally draining.

Best-case scenario if you do slip up, a handful of your contacts will quietly distance themselves. The worst case can get pretty crazy. Successful writers are a formidable bunch when provoked and that's not a fight you want to enter.

Within hours, an author's books can get bombarded with terrible reviews. That, in turn, can decimate their sales and stop algorithms recommending them. Once it starts, these same ranting writers often go down swinging until they've alienated everyone and are forced to change pen names or leave the industry.

All this could have been avoided if they separated their personal feelings from their professional persona. Being a professional doesn't mean changing who you are, but it can sometimes mean avoiding controversy and holding your tongue. Those who separate their personal and professional personas, on the whole, receive relatively little hatred, even as their social presence grows.

Of course, there are exceptions. It's impossible to avoid jealousy and controversy forever. However, those who don't bite back when things get heated and who focus on their work over personal drama are universally liked and respected. Do the same and your reputation will help you weather any storm.

Act in Good Faith

By comparison to most communities, authors are an inclusive and helpful bunch. It's unclear why this atmosphere of compassion evolved but my educated guess would point to the common lack of money shared by the vast majority. You see it often in poor real-world communities: in towns where success is rare, residents look out for their neighbours. Among authors, this means that those who do achieve success often feel the need to "pay it forward" – help those less fortunate, as they were once helped.

Having said that, this sentiment isn't universally ingrained. There are always individuals who will resort to more underhanded strategies to gain an unfair advantage.

For example, Stephen King is a household name and for good reason. His books have global appeal and have inspired more screen adaptations than any other author. A selection of books published online in 2016 bearing King's name, however, launched with comparatively lacklustre success. The reason was simple: they weren't written by the real Stephen King.

According to his website, someone has been "deceptively marketing and selling books by some other 'Stephen King'." The books were convincing imposters. So convincing, in fact, that thousands of avid King readers have been duped, allowing the fraudster to rake in a fortune while watering down the real Stephen King's reputation.

As you can imagine, the impersonator has stayed quiet, draining the scam for all it's worth while King's lawyers try to identify the individual responsible. The anonymous author has made no effort to network. However, if they tried, the backlash would probably be swift and unanimous. Intentionally sabotaging another writer's popularity by deceiving readers would undoubtedly lead to a short-term career.

Other authors have fessed up to having tried less controversial but equally selfish tactics. For example, a number have vented their irritation online when a marketing tactic they were exploiting but keeping quiet had become common knowledge and stopped working. While this seems wise, holding back information isn't the best way to keep friends or further your reputation, especially if your contacts have been generous with you. It's considered bad faith.

Doing the opposite, like six-figure authors Craig Martelle and Chris Fox, will earn you more influence. Both discovered early on that the military sci-fi sub-genre had an under-served audience of readers. Many in their position would have kept it to themselves, but not Martelle and Fox. As soon as they saw their books being rapidly devoured, they shared their discoveries: what worked, what didn't, and what might work well for others who wanted similar results.

As a result, they have become known for their results and respected for their transparency. They traded five minutes of domination, which would have eventually ended when others stumbled upon their secrets, for a lifetime of career opportunities.

In contrast, an infamous scandal in 2018 documented one author's fall from fortune when she tried the opposite. The scandal? *Cockygate*.

If you don't know the context, Cockygate started when successful romance author Faleena Hopkins wrote a series of romance books, each with the word "Cocky" in the title. On achieving success, she trademarked the word. It made sense from a business perspective. Corporations patent product ideas all the time to stop competitors copying them and leeching market share. If Faleena Hopkins quietly held onto her trademark to protect herself from imposters, like the fake Stephen King, she would have been fine. But that wasn't what happened.

She went on the attack.

You see, with intellectual property, it can be difficult to define what counts as infringement. Most people agree, though, that Hopkins crossed a line because she set out to remove *all* books from the market that used Cocky in their title, regardless of context. Because the term is widely used in romance books, this meant dozens of books by well-established authors were unpublished by online retailers after she contacted them. Instead of using her legal right to protect her assets, she used it as a weapon to remove her competition.

The backlash was swift. Within days, Hopkins left social media. Her name became a trending topic, her books were carpet-bombed with one-star reviews and her competitors sought to have her trademark revoked. Her networking potential nosedived and it took years to recover.

We're not here to judge the morality of either side. This example is simply meant to warn you that questionable tactics might gain you a short-term advantage, but they won't lead to lasting success. If you want to succeed in the networking game and maintain friendships that could lead to future opportunities, you need to adopt a long-term view. Sure, unsavoury actions today might grow your business but is the short-term gain worth a lifetime of professional enemies? A good reputation compounds over time and can lead to far more meaningful results.

GRADUATE TO DIRECT MESSAGES

Online, everyone starts out as a stranger. Getting those strangers to take a chance on you is fairly easy, particularly when they are also trying to network. What's not so easy is jumping from posting messages in a public forum to messaging contacts directly.

Doing so without knowing them personally feels intrusive but it is possible to make this step naturally. You start building your relationship in a public group by commenting on their posts (if you can add value or inspiration). If you see them interacting with your posts, you can intentionally bring them into conversations. For example, someone could ask:

What's the best way to market an audiobook?

In this case, your response would be:

I know **John Doe** did this recently. Any tips, John?

The fake author name in this example is presented in bold. That's because I've formatted it as it would appear on Facebook where you can comment a friend's name under a post and it becomes a clickable link. That person is notified that you've mentioned them. If you did this with Twitter, it would look more like:

I know @JohnDoe did this recently. Any tips, John?

The outcome is the same. The person tagged gets a notification telling them you've mentioned them and they can add their advice if they want. This message indicates that you pay attention to their work and it encourages them to show an interest in return.

If you do use this strategy, make sure the person you're including in conversations is relevant. Adding John Doe to an audiobook conversation, only to discover he's never produced one, would only work against you and demonstrate that you don't really know him. Shoehorning someone into a conversation with a tenuous link can be similarly damaging.

After you've shown that you know each other's work, direct messaging them with a follow-up question makes logical sense. It hasn't come out of the blue and can lead to fruitful conversations, collaboration, or general advice. It's part of building rapport.

Once you've made initial contact and had a one-to-one conversation, doing so again is easy. Done well and in moderation, direct messaging can be a great way to help turn a professional contact into a trusted friend.

MOVE TO EMAIL

Most professionals can be reached via email on their website's Contact page. It works like direct messages in that it creates a more intimate, one-to-one conversation. The benefits, however, don't stop there. When writing an email, you have far more formatting capabilities than you do on most social media platforms. You can add live links, create bullet points, insert images and attach files. This ability provides more enriching, nuanced conversations and makes it easier to explain ideas or projects.

Similar to direct messages, email can come across as intrusive if you don't know the recipient well, so proceed with caution. If they don't respond, drop it. If they do, don't overwhelm them with responses as that will only make them associate you with extra work and that will tarnish their perception of you. Remember, everyone's time is valuable and the more high-profile your contact is, the more their time comes at a premium.

Email sparingly and add as much value as possible in every message. That way, your effort will be noticed for the right reasons.

Be a Great Reader

It doesn't usually take a lot for two writers to get along. In most cases they have a lot in common. Writers who make a real connection, though, are those who know each other personally and each other's *work*. If you want to make an impression then research goes a long way, showing that you care enough to put in time and effort.

Many writers bypass reading a person's books in full by Googling them and scanning their titles and blurbs. They do enough to have a conversation but not enough to know the work in detail. That's fine. There aren't enough hours in a lifetime to read everything. But focusing on the flagship books by a select few authors can help your relationships blossom. It makes conversations more memorable and allows you to write a positive review online. Writers appreciate that extra effort because more social proof makes it easier for them to sell their books. In return, they're more likely to check out and recommend your work.

This strategy is labour intensive. But, as you develop your reputation, networking becomes less about casting a wide net to spread your name, and more about strategically targeting key individuals. Once you've gained experience, you can focus on the small proportion of your network that can deliver the greatest results. Then you can work less and get more done.

Get on Video

Nowadays, video plays a huge part in many authors' marketing plans but it can also be useful for networking. In fact, most authors should have a video presence somewhere online, whether it's YouTube, SnapChat, Facebook or somewhere else. The networking benefits are so powerful and multi-faceted, they're impossible to ignore.

For example, have you ever heard that a celebrity has died and felt genuine sadness despite having never met them? I certainly have. Steve Irwin, the Australian star of nature documentaries, was a big one for me. As a child I watched all his shows and absorbed his enthusiasm for animals. Even now I hear his voice every time I see his picture.

In the same vein, have you ever discovered that a celebrity you like supports a cause or business and have then become interested in it yourself because of their recommendation? Yeah, me too.

Now consider how many writers (those who were not already famous before they wrote books) have this effect. Few, I'd wager. Perhaps a handful: J K Rowling, Stephen King, Margaret Atwood.

The truth is, people know hundreds of singers, actors and talk-show hosts but few would recognise more than a handful of writers. And they almost certainly don't engage with them on an emotional level. The average reader could read a whole series of novels and still not spot the author in a line-up. Meanwhile, they would instantly jump into a conversation with their favourite movie star or musician and feel like they've known them for years.

Why is this?

Video.

No media replicates human connection more than seeing someone on a screen – whether it's via YouTube, Netflix or traditional TV. We are social creatures, programmed to develop emotional bonds based on factors including body language, voice intonation and facial expressions and a host of other non-verbal cues. Video fabricates a similar sensation to in-person talking even if we're not physically opposite the person speaking into the camera. The fact that we can see and hear them tricks our primitive brain into feeling as if we've met them. It's one of the few mediums, alongside audio-only alternatives, that can convey emotion and summon empathy.

Author Joanna Penn talks about this phenomenon on her YouTube channel. With a massive following, Penn admits that it's obviously impossible to know all her fans. However, they act as if they know her because they've watched her or listened to her for years. They remember her anecdotes and feel like they know how she likes to spend her time.

This is the impact broadcasting your face and voice can have. It helps your followers to feel they know you, even if you've never met. That's why video can establish your presence in a community.

Being today's most frequently shared type of content, video can also help to spread your reputation beyond your initial network. Before 2007, when YouTube ramped up video's mainstream appeal, text was king because it was easy to present on most digital devices. Jokes were spread in chain emails and words went viral. As technology developed, images followed. Memes became big business, with Grumpy Cat and Success Kid spreading rapidly. Now, in a world dominated by video and audio, YouTubers and podcasters have taken the throne.

With each video creating the impression that you've met someone, much of the groundwork of in-person introductions has been made far easier for keen networkers. As video content is shareable, any time you come up in conversation, someone in your network can introduce you to a new person within minutes – without any effort on your part – by sharing your video.

Video truly is an amazing, scalable networking strategy. And the best part? The more you are shared, the more popular you become... and the more you are shared. It's a virtuous circle!

The type of content you will want to produce will depend on your end goal. If you want to grow an audience of fiction readers, you could start by becoming a BookTuber – reviewing your favourite books on YouTube, which are hopefully in the same genre as the books you write. This will attract both readers and other authors who work in that genre, keen to get you to review their books.

Alternatively, you might want to vlog (video blog) your journey through the writing process and publication, sharing your mistakes and successes. Again, this will appeal to readers who like to peek behind the publishing curtain and see how their favourite books are created. However, it will also attract other writers who want to follow your trajectory and find out what you did that went well to minimise their own mistakes. You don't have to be polished and professional with this type of content. In non-fiction, knowing your mistakes and pitfalls can be just as interesting to your audience and contacts as finding out what worked. You'll be all the more respected for practicing a candid approach to both.

As your platform and expertise grow, you could then move on to more structured content. This could mean talking about your latest book releases, interviewing your editor or running a general Q&A. All are valid forms of video content that will make you a more attractive and approachable contact in the author networking world.

Fame for fame's sake isn't the goal, but the momentum of building popularity certainly helps you to meet ever-larger influencers. Establishing a video presence on a platform of your choice could provide the initial push you need.

COLLABORATE

Collaboration comes in many forms and each of them can help you to deepen relationships.

If you want to cosy up to a distributor, you might give them an exclusivity period when you release a new book. That's collaboration. If you're interested in working with a particular artist, it could mean adapting your work as a graphic novel and splitting the royalties 50/50. Also collaboration. Or you could co-write a novel or co-create an anthology with authors in the same genre and pool your resources for a big launch. There are lots of ways to collaborate.

Whatever option you choose, it is almost certain to kickstart a strong bond with collaborators. Many writers nurture this process by meeting on a regular basis to develop their shared project. However, a physical meeting is no longer necessary. In the not-too-distant past, creatives would only work together if they lived close by (or, at the very least, they needed to talk on the phone) so were limited by time zone differences and snail mail delays.

Not anymore.

On the internet, information can be sent thousands of miles in seconds. Video-chat technology like Skype and Zoom means creators can meet in the digital world and convey most of the nuances of a face-to-face conversation, even hold up drawings to the camera or share their screens to flesh out ideas. It has made collaboration among distant contacts more achievable and popular.

In some cases, barriers like time zones have actually been advantageous. Joanna Penn has talked about her collaborations with J Thorn on her podcast. Together, they have worked on two books. While one was conducted during a physical journey together with two other authors, their first venture happened while on separate continents.

This distance was used to their advantage. Their novel consisted of alternate chapters from separate character perspectives. While Thorn was asleep, Penn wrote a chapter. Then Thorn read Penn's chapter and wrote his next one while she was asleep. The different time zones meant they worked on the book continuously, neither having to wait for the other. Neither made excuses for missing a deadline because they knew the other would hold them accountable the next morning.

Co-writing won't be the best idea for all authors, particularly rookies who haven't yet found their voice. In that case, paying an editor to help you improve your craft would be a better option than seeking out a co-writer. That said, if you already have a good track record as a writer, collaborating to develop a close working friendship might be a good networking opportunity.

If you have time, you could organise a collaboration of multiple authors. Anthology organisers shoulder a huge portion of the workload. They project-manage up to 20 authors, plus write a contribution themselves, but they also gain the most benefit.

I was part of a project like this in 2018. We all worked hard but the organiser and lead author, Andy Peloquin, was run ragged. As a result of his central role, he became well respected and went on to have greater commercial success than the rest of us for several months following the book's launch.

This happened because, on certain online bookstores, books are ranked and organised into bestseller charts and so are authors. An author's rank is based on overall book sales plus other factors such as the revenue their books generate, and the amount of "read-through" (repeat customers buying sequels) they receive.

In this case, Peloquin set up a promotion for his own books while working hard with his collaborators to send the anthology high into the charts. As a result, he saw over $10,000 of royalties pass through his Kindle Direct Publishing account in one month, catapulting him onto a list of the world's top 100 bestselling fantasy authors. That extra exposure enabled him to benefit from a sales halo where readers bought his other titles.

Collaboration can deepen your close relationships and catapult your reputation. How you fare depends on how you collaborate as each case comes with its own benefits.

SHARE YOUR BEST IDEAS

You often hear veteran authors say you should never hold back anything from your current project. I wholeheartedly agree. Yet newer authors commonly fixate on the notion that they should store their best ideas for later books to show a development in their work.

This mindset suggests that they believe their current ideas are the best they will ever have, which is flawed logic. If anything, creative minds produce ideas faster than they can act upon them, meaning you have more ideas to choose from over time. On top of that, you hopefully get better at executing them.

That's why holding back your best ideas for a third, fifth or tenth book is a bad strategy. Start too small and you risk losing your readers before they see your best work. Really, who wants a debut novel full of second-rate concepts? Readers don't care about author development. They want awesome stories, book after book. Many won't read them in order anyway.

In the same vein, new and veteran authors alike commonly express the opinion that revealing their best secrets to fellow authors means giving too much power to their competition. Whether it's revealing an under-served pocket of hungry readers, or a fresh marketing tactic, they keep their secrets and ladle out vague advice.

Indie authors have bucked this trend, having learned that few people discover something alone. While one lone wolf is testing an idea, there are always others following the same line of enquiry without knowing it. Unconnected minds get similar ideas. If you don't share your discovery, someone else will, usually while plugging a paid course. The savviest entrepreneurs know that the early-adopter gravy train eventually runs dry and those who benefit most usually either come out well by helping a lot of people and collecting social karma, or by selling what they know.

Just look at the biggest revolutions in publishing over the last few years, including the rapid release strategy and the idea of writers licensing out universes, which I'll explain. These have come from authors who once held a secret that was working for them. Those secrets have now become common practice. The authors whose names have lasted over time are those who broke the news.

Liliana Hart is a successful crime and romance author who has maintained a lucrative writing business since becoming successful during the early days of self-publishing on Amazon. She discovered the "Liliana Nirvana" – a term that has evolved into the ubiquitous rapid release strategy. The idea involves withholding finished books until you can release three to five within a few weeks of each other. That way, you benefit from multiple titles entering the charts and cross-selling each other in a short timeframe.

Likewise, Michael Anderle revealed that writing multiple book series within one fictional universe was good for business as each new instalment promoted previous releases. As more authors join his brand, each one gets access to a host of knowledgeable contacts while contributing their own creativity to help the cause.

Brian Meeks mastered Amazon ads and has become a staple on podcasts and stages around the world.

Mark Dawson popularised the idea of using Facebook ads to sell books and has evolved into one of the biggest names in the industry.

None of these people lost their competitive advantage by sharing their best information. If anything, those who didn't share ended up losing out because they didn't capitalise on what they knew and use it to grow their reputation.

The educators who taught the information gained a financial and status boost from being tied to these strategies, which led to more opportunities. Large companies have used them as consultants. They've been allowed to test innovative marketing tools before their peers. Plus, they've had opportunities to talk to some of the most influential figures in the industry, including Big Five publishers and Amazon executives. All the while, they have continued to live generously and use the respect and kudos gained from their generosity to attract more success.

Living by example and sharing their best ideas has offered them these fantastic opportunities. What's more, their ideas have never run dry. If you want to wow potential connections with the value you deliver, sharing you best ideas is a good way to become memorable and respected. It won't make your journey harder. On the contrary, whether the information you share regards marketing, publicity, collaboration opportunities or something else, you're not creating stronger competition; you're creating stronger allies. And that's something that will ultimately benefit you.

Online relationships are easier to initiate than face-to-face ones but harder to nurture due to the obvious lack of personal interaction. However, if you follow the advice outlined here and remain proactive, you can achieve a long-lasting foothold in the industry without ever having to leave home.

Actions to Take

When it comes to strengthening online relationships:

- ✓ Build a reputation over the long term
- ✓ Work hard and remain enthusiastic to maintain contacts
- ✓ Post consistently to stay well-known and benefit from social media algorithms
- ✓ Act professionally to avoid alienation
- ✓ Avoid controversial topics to keep a diverse range of friendships
- ✓ Remain civil at all times and accept constructive criticism with grace
- ✓ Act in good faith
- ✓ Use emails and direct messages to deepen bonds with important contacts
- ✓ Read and review your peers' work to show you care
- ✓ Get on video to be seen as a real person rather than just a profile picture
- ✓ Collaborate to involve other creative entrepreneurs in your success
- ✓ Share your best advice to benefit your reputation rather than seeking short-term advantages
- ✓ Work consistently to stay visible

NETWORKING
IN THE
REAL WORLD

8

WAYS TO NETWORK OFFLINE

Remember when you were a kid at a family party or barbeque? The adults would get together with their friends and you would tag along with their assurance that it would be fun. When you first arrived, you wouldn't know any of the other families' kids. None went to your school or lived in your neighbourhood so you'd stay quiet and stick close to your parents' legs until someone invited you to play.

Eventually, you'd get over that initial shyness and talk. Within hours, those strange, unfamiliar kids would graduate to good friends. You'd completely lose yourself, chasing imaginary aliens across the lawn, armed with water pistols and tennis-ball grenades, laughing and yelling as if you'd been raised together. When the time finally arrived to go home, you'd beg to stay for a sleepover because you were having so much fun.

Afterwards, every time your parents talked about visiting again, you would flood with excitement. You'd get to see your new friends again! You'd get to play in the garden and, maybe, sleep over! All this, despite only having met them once.

Ah, the innocence of childhood. Every challenge seemed so big yet each was overcome with so little emotional friction. As adults, you'd think we'd be better equipped to tackle the same challenges. To make firm friends in one meeting as we did as a child, particularly if those friends had a lot in common with us. Yet, we don't cope quite as well as we would hope.

As children, many of us would spend much of our free time playing with new kids, limited only by how far our parents let us stray. Despite having our own money and freedom as adults, however, our social circles typically get smaller. We leave education and get a job. Time restraints force us to decide whether to make new friendships or nurture already-neglected existing ones. And, over time, we find our circle decreasing as our friends start families and follow careers, just as busy as us.

It's a result of circumstance, but our brains often fool us into thinking we aren't as good at making new friends as we once were. We reinforce this belief by behaving in a way that ensures we never branch out: we turn down invitations from acquaintances – stopping ourselves from getting to know them because we don't *already* know them. Then we tell ourselves we didn't get to know them because we couldn't.

We create self-fulfilling prophecies, acting in ways that justify our excuses until we believe them. We tell ourselves that we *can't* make new friends quickly when we can. It's just that we stay guarded, sticking to our gradually dwindling social circles, and never give ourselves the opportunity to prove ourselves otherwise.

Knowing that this isn't reality, that we are social creatures capable of making friends as adults, is a mindset shift that's key to succeeding when networking in person. Once you've overcome that hurdle, networking changes from a chore into something that excites you.

Personally, I love networking. Entering a room full of likeminded individuals thrills me. You'd be surprised how quickly you find yourself sitting with a new friend and creating inside jokes when your lifestyles are so relatable. We like to think we're unique, especially as creatives, but we're more similar than we care to admit. In networking, that's a good thing!

Let's look at an example to understand why.

I spend lots of time working at home, lost in my own world, writing while listening to audio tracks of thunder or coffee shop background noises through my headphones. To the average person, this isn't normal behaviour. Not only do they not understand why someone would rather listen to the whir of a coffee percolator than music (the lyrics distract me) but they also don't accept that writing time is precious. They don't get that, while enjoyable, it requires discipline. They think it's easy.

"As you're not doing much, do you mind helping me with...?"

"*You've* had a hard day? You've spent the past six hours playing on your laptop!"

Sound familiar? The truth is, many people believe they know what it's like to write a book, but few are dedicated enough to know how much work it takes. Even fewer become full-time authors that treat their writing as a career.

They don't like or understand the *real* writer's lifestyle – the wordcount targets, repetitive strain injuries and staring at a screen or page for hours on end. They just like the *idea* of it perpetuated by fiction, where authors attend book signings and black-tie award ceremonies.

A tiny proportion of the population are professional writers so the chances of two meeting randomly are slim. Attending networking events doesn't mean you will only talk to full-timers but they do bring together a significant concentration of people who share their obsession and mentality.

As a result, it's easy to find kindred spirits. Conversations flow, friendships are made, nicknames and inside jokes are formed. Attendees become relevant to one another in ways that would never have happened had they kept their relationship purely online.

These meetups are invaluable because you can form bonds but also read emotions as you press upon different topics. You can actually see people's pain points and interests and work out how to add value to your peers' lives.

Sounds ideal, doesn't it? Build your professional network while expanding your friendship circle. Well, it can be. The tricky part is bridging the gap between chatting online and sharing a coffee with a new friend.

Luckily, this section will fill in the gaps, revealing steps you can take and places where you can make the transition. Follow this advice and you'll soon be having a blast at events.

Avoid Business Networking Groups

To many people, particularly those coming from the corporate world, it will make logical sense to sign up to a traditional business networking group. That's networking 101, isn't it? Not in this case.

Traditional networking groups can provide fantastic opportunities for business owners in many industries but they aren't necessarily the best investment choice for authors, unless you write non-fiction books on, say, management. Many, like the leading organisation, Business Network International (BNI), have hundreds of thousands of members globally and provide opportunities to meet other members in person and online. However, membership costs a significant annual fee and you are unlikely to meet other authors or even publishers.

If you are an author coach, or provide editing services, then you *can* gain value from such a group because many business owners want to write a book or have copy-writing requirements and will pay for your expertise. However, if your intention is to enter a flourishing author ecosystem, this is probably not the route for you.

UNPAID WORK EXPERIENCE AND INTERNSHIPS

Not everyone wants to take on another job to build a network. Some people don't want to be a full-time writer or work in the publishing industry. To them, writing is a hobby. They simply want their hobby to be a little more sociable.

Many people also don't want to be an indie author and learn how to control the whole publishing and distribution process. Their dream is to be published by Penguin Random House and sign books that are sent to them. That's fine too.

The advice in this chapter will still be relevant to you if that's the case. However, you might use it to improve your chances of getting a deal rather than publishing yourself. Personally, I chose the latter and it helped tremendously.

Initially, it started when I contacted David Norrington at Wordcatcher Publishing, offering free editorial work as a publishing assistant. Large companies get these sorts of offers on a frequent basis – they rely on internships to maintain profits – but small companies typically get overlooked. The fact that they don't publish Stephen King, however, doesn't mean they aren't worth joining. For a start, small companies tend to give you a more varied role, meaning you learn more on the job than you would somewhere bigger.

If you can do it, getting a part-time publishing internship will grant you access to a ready-made network of contacts that can save you time building relationships in the long term. In my experience, I learned editing, formatting and marketing skills while getting to meet booksellers, printers, other publishers, cover designers and writers. It was fantastic!

If you can get paid, consider that a bonus but remember, you don't have to hold down that job forever. The aim isn't making money that way. It's meeting people and learning what they know. If you're an indie, the added education you receive is a bonus.

SWITCH CAREERS

This is a more extreme method but it can work wonders, allowing you to immerse yourself in the industry full-time. Many writers starting out do this to kickstart their network, by starting their own business aimed at publishers, or switching jobs to one that exists in a publishing or publishing-services company.

I've encountered marketers who have done this, along with accountants, programmers, journalists, designers and copywriters. They aren't publishers in the traditional sense but they have positioned themselves to work with people who have skills that are useful in their author network. In doing so, they have a reason to keep in touch with them in a physical setting and develop rapport.

MEET UP WITH STRANGERS YOU MET ONLINE

"You want me to do what?!" I know. Either you were warned about this as a child or you've repeated this warning hundreds of times to children yourself.

Hear me out. As a child, "don't talk to strangers on the internet" is good advice. The internet is full of dangerous weirdos and they've worked out a range of ways to hide their true identities until it's too late.

As an adult, the internet can still be a dangerous place but the "don't meet strangers" rules aren't quite so straightforward. In the words of Captain Barbosa from Disney's *Pirates of the Caribbean,* "They're more like guidelines."

Ultimately, when meeting new acquaintances, common sense should prevail. It's possible to strike a balance between being sensible and jumping on opportunities. This suggestion might upset the ingrained paranoia from childhood but meeting strangers from the internet is now considered the new networking norm. Not only that, it's the most effective way to weed out those who aren't serious. Someone can claim to be anything they want while hidden behind an alias. But it's difficult to keep up the charade when they're sitting in a circle of knowledgeable, well-connected professionals.

It's easy to find good networking prospects on the internet. I've met people in the real world after first talking to them on Facebook, Twitter and the comment sections of blog posts.

Other authors I know have met collaborators on the story-sharing site Wattpad and through Instagram. As long as you meet these strangers at conferences or writers' circles – anywhere public to ensure your safety – getting together in the real world with relevant professionals you met online can lead to fruitful relationships.

As most networking professionals are easily searchable online these days, authors often pre-organise meetings with potential collaborators ahead of events. It's safer that way when you think about it. What's the alternative? Meeting strangers by chance with no prior information? That's how it would once have happened. It's dumbfounding that many otherwise rational adults see that as a safer option, just because it doesn't mean meeting someone "from the internet."

The world has changed. According to *The Economist*: "today dating sites and apps count for about a sixth of the first meetings that lead to marriage." Nowadays, teenagers meet close friends online in gaming communities. Students search for whoever has been assigned the same accommodation block as them before heading to university. Professionals in all industries check which of their connections are attending events before deciding to buy a ticket themselves.

It's no longer a place where chatroom friends stay anonymous and real friends are people you meet at a bar. Social media is so all-encompassing that our online personas and real-life identities have become blurred.

If being targeted by a dangerous stranger is your concern, then networking events should be the least of your worries. Many people who see you in the street can find your online profiles and work out roughly where you live. SnapChat broadcasts your location on a regular basis. Facebook friends can check you into tourist hotspots when you're with them. Your Instagram posts are a catalogue of backdrops showing where you've been.

Your personal security is compromised on a near-constant basis. The only difference with meeting individuals you already know online is that there's a breadcrumb trail of evidence linking them to your life and location. If anything, that evidence means you're more protected meeting them than meeting a random stranger you've never spoken to before.

If you're still uncomfortable meeting online contacts then there's a simple solution: take a friend.

AUTHOR EVENTS

Various factors dictate which events authors can attend. For example, if you live in Siberia, you're unlikely to find outdoor gatherings in your area. Likewise, you won't find successful conferences anywhere that has terrible transport links. Nor will you be able to justify attending an event internationally if you aren't yet selling lots of books. All these things can limit your ability to attend an event. However, that doesn't mean you can't network effectively.

Sci-fi author Craig Martelle lives in remote Alaska. Despite this apparent drawback he has become one of the best-connected authors on the planet, organising some of the world's biggest author networking events in Las Vegas, Bali, Edinburgh and London. His openness and selflessness have broadened access to all who know him and call him friend.

Clearly, this works for him because he's a competent entrepreneur, but it won't necessarily align with your vision. Thankfully, this section has options for everyone. Browsing the following choices should help you plan a networking strategy that suits your nature and goals.

WRITERS' GROUPS

Writers' groups are a good place for newbie authors to start networking. The ones I've visited have been full of writers at various stages in their careers, from complete beginners to award-winning novelists, although this is uncommon.

The reason they make such a good place to start is because they focus on developing you as an author. There doesn't have to be any pretence of being an expert: you're there to learn. The whole point is to turn up with work you want to see critiqued and improved. Networking is a secondary benefit.

The people you meet at these groups can be a mixed bag. You won't often find bestsellers amongst their ranks but that doesn't necessarily matter. If you're a newbie, the purpose is to learn and meet people. The close ranks and small numbers make starting conversation and establishing connections easy.

As writers' groups usually consist of small numbers, more established writers tend to prefer to focus on larger venues with a wider range of connections. Likewise, if you already have lots of strong online contacts and a proven track record as an author, this might not be the venue for you.

Writers' groups are great. Some established writers love the accountability they provide, but most use them as a place to develop their craft and learn the ropes among more experienced hobbyist writers. Then they move on.

That's not to say there aren't groups with extremely professional members. This is only something I've noticed after attending circles across the UK that contained mainly hobbyists. No judgement; just an observation to help you strategise.

If you're shy, or a new face on the publishing scene, a good writers' group is the perfect place to start your journey. Just make sure to judge the room before you try to steer the conversation towards business or craft. Every group is different and many have been running for decades. Some like to focus purely on craft whereas others don't mind discussing marketability and publishing.

The best way to make the most of any group is to adhere to their rules and to add to the experience rather than attempt to change it.

WORKSHOPS

A workshop aims to improve an aspect of your knowledge. What aspect that is depends on its agenda. Training invariably requires a fee but, if the host has a good track record, paying for their wisdom and knowledge can be a fantastic deal.

The benefits are fourfold:

1.   Quality information
2.   High-calibre attendees
3.   A well-connected teacher
4.   Healthy competition

On average, the quality of attendees is going to be high because they value education enough to pay for it. This means they have a growth mindset, which is a common trait among high achievers and a great signal to watch out for when networking. Those with a growth mindset are typically driven, curious and positive. They aren't afraid to fail because they recognise failure as part of the learning process.

Sharing a class with these people nurtures camaraderie, breaks the ice and forces you to interact. Depending on the course content, it can even attract entrepreneurs that could fill the various roles on your networking dream team.

Learning as a team makes success more likely as attendees can draw on each others' help as well as that of the tutor. Plus, competition between classmates adds a healthy dose of accountability that keeps you motivated.

Many authors start out this way only to realise years later, when they hit a bestseller list, that other alumni have achieved similar success. While striving, they used their desire to be the most successful member to keep them motivated. Workshops provide a great opportunity to start these relationships with future stars early in your career and are a reason to stay in touch. Then, as they rise in success, each member can access the connections others have made to reach new heights.

Additionally, there's the teacher to consider. Typically, the individuals who run these workshops have extensive experience and have accumulated valuable friends along the way. Their course content is useful. However, you can learn more from them than what's on the curriculum.

The class might be on developing your authorial voice but that doesn't mean you can't ask other questions: applying to publishers, what agents they know, other students looking to co-write a book in your genre, etc. Don't derail the class. That would be disrespectful to the tutor and attendees who want to learn the course content they are expecting. If you are disruptive, the tutor won't share the information you seek. Plus, your classmates won't want to stay in contact. But do consider asking about things that aren't taught on the curriculum if you think they could lead to opportunities.

Not everything you gain from a workshop will necessarily appear on the itinerary if you know how turn a one-day event into long-term relationships.

BOOK SIGNINGS

Ones conducted by other authors, not yours.

Book signings are commonly held in bookstores but they can be anywhere. Several authors I know have done hundreds of signings, and venues have included bookshops, supermarkets, school halls, fêtes, art galleries, libraries, theatres, bars, and even a castle. There are hundreds of potential places to run into an author signing books.

The best way to capitalise on such meetings, I've found, is to carry business cards everywhere. Big-name authors sometimes run book signings with an entourage and have little time to chat to individual readers, with hundreds waiting behind them. Unknown writers, by contrast, usually encourage connections and will keep your details.

Approaching them with curiosity and enthusiasm can help you to introduce yourself as a fellow author. Buying one of their books also shows good faith. Nothing puts you in an author's good books more than buying one of their latest releases.

The advantage of going to signings is that you know the writer you're talking to is definitely published and connected in some way, if only to the person who owns the venue. Therefore, they're a quality contact.

Handing them your card and asking for their details is a great way to follow up on the conversation. If you buy their book, let them know if you plan to post a review. This offer can instantly put you on good terms.

Book Fairs

There are two types of book fair. Some, like The London Book Fair or Book Expo America, are trade shows for publishing professionals, where all sorts of related businesses and professional visitors congregate to network, educate, learn and do business together. For the purpose of this book, we'll refer to these as "conferences."

True book fairs, in this context, are reader-focused affairs, like the Hay Festival. As a guest, you can watch authors, artists and actors speak on a range of subjects. Or you can simply lay on the grass and read a novel you bought from a local bookshop.

Smaller examples exist too, but they're not as famous. You know the sort: bunting, a bake sale and a town hall full of authors, each with their own stall. Most will look like this, unless you live in a large city where your local book fair has an entry fee and a corporate sponsor.

Regardless of how they're packaged, these events are invaluable to writers. Note that I didn't say they're great for selling books. While some of the bigger book fairs can lead to hundreds of sales, most smaller ones will rarely result in selling enough books to cover your table fee and travel expenses. If sales are your goal, you're better off investing your time and money on advertising.

Book fairs are, however, great networking opportunities. On the day, they work a lot like speed dating, where lulls in visitor footfall become opportunities to visit your fellow vendors, typically with a cupcake from the bake sale.

While doing an initial sweep of the tables, I make a mental note of those I find interesting then circle back later for more details. You're unlikely to meet many A-listers at these events but they have a strong sense of community, with some attendees returning each year. Most are happy to talk.

CRAFT FAIRS

Craft fairs look indistinguishable from book fairs: their organisers often share the same enthusiasm for community and the same unhealthy but loveable obsession with bunting. Yet, there's one key difference; the focus isn't on books. This means there are likely to be fewer authors but a wider draw for visitors. Whole families arrive to browse artisan stalls run by all manner of local creatives.

You might think this sort of event will hold fewer networking opportunities. Think again. Do you need cover art? There's almost certainly a local illustrator standing in line at the ice cream van, or with a stand of their own. Or you could chat to the photographer perched near the raffle. Need props for your book-signing setup? The sculptor makes wooden wizards that match your fantasy novels. Selling them at signings would provide you with an extra revenue stream. Do you want to set up your own book fair? The councillor who holds the keys to the community centre is propped up against a picnic bench. The fact that he has his face painted like a tiger is irrelevant. Go and talk to him. He won't bite! These places can provide valuable contacts.

COFFEE SHOPS AND BARS

Writers gather for many reasons. Sometimes they want specific advice on writing. Other times they want marketing tactics, or to be kept accountable. Then there are those who need an excuse to get out of the house and talk to people who understand their lifestyle.

Coffee shops and bars are fantastic places to host these gatherings. It's usually easy to find one in most towns and villages. Cities have even more options.

Typically, these meetups start with authors who already know each other but they are open to new members. You just have to figure out how to contact them through Facebook or local libraries. Adverts are sometimes posted on the notice board of social hubs like dentists' waiting rooms, community centres, etc.

If you would like to join, simply contact a member to find out when the group is next planning to gather and ask if you can take part. That way they'll be expecting you and will introduce you to the group. This is a speedy way to find friends who meet regularly.

WRITERS' WALKS

Writers' walks have come into vogue in recent years, spawned from the discovery that a large proportion of writers also enjoy endurance hiking. It's unclear why this is. Possibly, it's the low cost that draws them, or something to do with having the type of mind that thrives on a long-distance goal.

Regardless of how it came about, you can find examples from history and the modern day: William Wordsworth, Charles Dickens and Jim Butcher are a few notable writers who publicly commented on the merits of walking. This sentiment has stuck with the writing community through the ages.

As a result, some intrepid writers have combined the two passions, encouraging writers to chat while they explore the countryside. A few even buddy-up as running mates for ultramarathons. If you're a writer who loves to sweat outdoors, this option could help you to get some exercise, meet friends and build your publishing network.

WRITERS' CONFERENCES

Arguably the most value-packed of all writerly events, writers' conferences usually attract authors from across a spectrum of abilities and success levels. They are typically held in hotels, conference centres or stadium-sized buildings as part of trade shows where publishing services companies and sponsors come together.

There are some fantastic ones around the world. With prominent conferences and festivals in most developed countries, it's impossible to fit them all here without overwhelming this chapter with a list spanning several pages. However, some good conferences to check out as a starting point include:

- o   The Smarter Artist Summit in the US
- o   The London Book Fair in the UK
- o   Bologna Children's Book Fair in Italy
- o   BookExpo America in the US
- o   The Sell More Books Show Summit in the US
- o   The Hay Festival in the UK
- o   20Books Edinburgh in the UK and Vegas in the US
- o   Hong Kong Book Fair in Hong Kong
- o   Beijing International Book Fair in China
- o   Novelists Inc. in the US
- o   Vancouver Writers Fest in Canada
- o   Frankfurt Book Fair in Germany
- o   FutureBook Live in the UK

Savvy, well-connected writers gravitate to these events because they know how much value a chance encounter can yield. They all have different focuses so researching which ones will provide the most value to your business is crucial.

For instance, some revolve around the subject of technology and the internet, like the Smarter Artist Summit or FutureBook Live. Others, like Bologna, explore the children's market in depth. Beijing, while international in nature, tends to focus on China's huge English and translation markets. Hong Kong and the Hay Festival are more about serving readers than industry professionals, far more than some of the other events. As for Novelists Inc. and the 20Books conferences, they draw a lot of self-published authors so talks tend to me more indie in nature.

If you want a more comprehensive list of conferences with details on locations, dates, visitor numbers and subject matter, you can find them at:

DanielParsonsBooks.com/Networking

Throughout the course of each event, various expert speakers (usually successful authors, heads of major companies and creative innovators) deliver talks and seminars, take questions, and encourage opportunities for guests to mingle.

Historically, writers' conferences were small affairs, commonly bolted onto larger traditional conferences and trade shows for publishers and agents. Nowadays, these conferences are juggernauts in their own right. As self-publishing has clawed more market share and become an increasingly viable option for authors, it has developed considerable clout. On top of that, events have expanded to cater for a wider range of business models including traditional publishing and hybrid publishing for authors who work in a variety of ways.

At The London Book Fair, the trend is impossible to miss. *The Author HQ*, a section once reserved for in-the-know writers, has grown substantially over the last few years. It now attracts thousands of interested people and a fleet of author-servicing businesses and sponsors. Likewise, indie afterparties have become so popular that organisers, who once joined forces to pool their authors, need to separate their parties because the bars can't manage the numbers. Some attendees are so in-demand they attend multiple parties each night.

A few organisers have taken the idea of giving writers their own conferences even further and left the shadow of their larger, traditional publishing partners. In early 2019, 20BooksTo50K's Vegas convention sold out 850 tickets in 30 minutes. Authors were willing to pay hundreds of dollars plus travel to be there.

Conferences are growing in size and complexity as authors' businesses mature. For this reason, conferences will be our primary focus for the next few chapters.

A NOTE ON LIMITS

One paradox that virtual and physical networking spaces share is that they are simultaneously limitless and full of limits. You can talk to *anyone* but some conversations require luck, circumstance or cash to get involved. Venues have space limits but that's not all an ambitious author has to face.

Subscription-only author communities such as the Alliance of Independent Authors (ALLi) host events that are free to attend, primarily to attract new members. However, that isn't the case with every organisation.

Novelists Inc. (NINC) is a professional conference hosted in Florida, USA. The organisers pride themselves on creating an event that delivers value for authors with further advanced careers. Speakers present on complex topics that many new authors might struggle to understand. Thus, NINC imposes requirements that visitors must meet to attend. This entails having two published novels (each 30,000 words or longer, not part of an anthology) and generating $2,000 in royalties in the past 12 months via traditional publishing methods, or $5,000 self-published. As the high-calibre attendees value their time, these requirements filter attendees. This means speakers aren't bogged down with basic questions and can spend more time discussing advanced strategies.

Other events demand different criteria for access. For example, the world's largest writers' conferences now attract Amazon representatives and stands manned by big-name authors who share their success stories to inspire new writers. Typically, the company hosts an evening drinks session where they invite their guest stars, who are often published by them, as well as rising stars who have made it onto their radar. The requirement here isn't how much money you've made; it's whether you get an invitation, and that depends on whether Amazon's traditional publishing imprints are interested in signing you.

A final barrier to entry is your bank balance. Some networking conferences cater only for the heavy-hitters. Hosted by Craig Martelle in 2018, the non-profit organisation 20BooksTo50K held an event that screamed exclusivity. Set on the beach in Bali, it was intended to be for six-figure authors. It was possible to attend if you were a little short of that number, as this requirement wasn't rigidly enforced. However, at over $3,000 per person, the ticket price filtered out most hopefuls, even if it did include hotel accommodation, speakers' fees and various other perks.

Sounds expensive? Well, not when you consider how much the attendees earned – some as much at $3,000 *per day*! Bali was a one-time conference designed to celebrate success as much as it was about learning. When you consider that you're rubbing shoulders with some of the industry's elite authors, the price tag seems almost insignificant.

The right deal could generate enough money in royalties to cover the average salary for years. Urban fantasy author Elaine Bateman (E G Bateman) attended and got a nine-book co-writing deal with Michael Anderle, one of the world's most popular writers, despite not having hit the six-figure benchmark herself at the time.

Across the board, conferences have entry barriers and newbies definitely won't have the same opportunities that are available to long-term networkers. However, that doesn't mean you can't get there. The truth is, everyone has to start somewhere. As you learn, grow, make more powerful friends and learn to navigate more exclusive social circles, things will get easier.

Not every specific opportunity you want will open up to you. Even J K Rowling isn't *guaranteed* an audience at the White House. That's just how the world works. But you will be able to achieve most goals, even if help comes from a different group than the one you expected. One lesson you can learn from this harsh reality is that a game plan can open up the *right* opportunities. Want to be considered for a literary award? You'll need to know literary critics and probably spend money to enter, depending on the award. Want to earn oodles of cash? Try seeking out the titans of your genre. Your time on this Earth is limited so you can't do *everything* but you can do *anything*, so long as you put in the work.

To start, write down a list of the things you want from your career and reverse engineer a strategy to meet the *type* of people you need to achieve them. For example, to get your books featured at the front of a national bookstore chain:

1. Talk to their regional or national book buyer and find out if you can set up a distribution deal. If not…
2. Find out which publishers they buy from that publish books in your genre.
3. Scour the publisher's website for a relevant commissioning editor.
4. Contact that editor online or at a public event to find out which literary agents already have a relationship with them.
5. Aim to meet that agent in-person at a public event or pitch to them via the normal channels.

There often isn't just one person standing between you and a goal. In many cases, multiple conversations and relationships are required to achieve what you want, but a goal is almost always possible. All it takes is the right combination of contacts.

Don't worry if you don't know every detail from the beginning. As more of the world lights up for you, you will learn about the existence of people you might never have considered, new paths and options will arise, and new opportunities will present themselves.

Actions to Take

When meeting industry contacts in person:

- ✓ Know that adults can make friends as quickly as kids
- ✓ Understand that real interaction leads to better bonds
- ✓ Expand your personal social circle, not just your business
- ✓ Avoid traditional business networks as a new author
- ✓ Consider switching careers to get started
- ✓ Meet strangers from the internet
- ✓ Take a friend if internet strangers scare you
- ✓ Attend or organise events no matter where you live
- ✓ Try writers' groups if you're a newbie
- ✓ Attend workshops to learn and make connections
- ✓ Meet other authors at book signings
- ✓ Think of local book fairs as networking hotspots
- ✓ Be creative at craft fairs and fêtes
- ✓ Find author clubs that meet at coffee shops and bars
- ✓ Try writers' walks if you want to exercise and make connections
- ✓ Focus most of your effort on conferences because they provide the most opportunities
- ✓ Assess your priorities and plan ahead to network in circles that align with your goals

9

ADDRESSING PRE-EVENT CONCERNS

So, we know lots of places we could be networking. Most of the information from this point on will concentrate on writers' conferences because they are the most useful networking events for authors. However, the advice will apply to *any* potential networking situation. Indeed, much of what we will explore are transferrable skills and can be applied in many situations.

We will begin by developing a positive mindset for networking in the physical world. This is the best place to start because being proactive will help you later. Whether you have chronic insecurities or just over-analyse your actions, a mindset slip could occur at any point. Training yourself to anticipate one can help you avoid derailing your progress with impulsive reactions.

Preparation can also teach you not to exaggerate others' reactions in your imagination and instead consider their more realistic thoughts. Only by knowing how to handle any potential stumbling blocks can you make calculated moves to protect yourself against self-sabotage.

This section will take you through common concerns writers have before attending an event. Exploring each one, we will unpick your rationale and apply wisdom to ease your anxiety. In so doing, you can get on with your strategy unhindered and start adding new friends to your network.

"I Can't Do This, I'm an Introvert!"

Most people don't like meeting new people. They also consider themselves introverted to some degree. Confidence is dependent on the situation for most people, so it makes sense.

Believe it or not, I class myself primarily as an introvert. From childhood to my late teens, I was extremely shy. However, I don't struggle with social interactions now because my school teachers were great coaches. They believed in immersion therapy – the idea that exposing yourself to a phobia eventually desensitises you to it. Hence, I had to do lots of presentations and group work, which over time taught me to manage my fear. I still get nervous if I have to talk in front of a crowd but not to the same extent.

The same strategy can be applied to networking. At first, you might attend a group meetup with butterflies and nausea. But those feelings won't last long if you take a breath, immerse yourself in the experience and get talking. In many cases, you'll find that you're more capable of holding a conversation with a stranger than you thought.

Plus, it's not solely your responsibility to carry the conversation. Remember, conversations include more than one person, which means that there will always be someone else to pick up the slack if you find yourself floundering. Nobody wants a bad conversation, particularly in a networking session, so everyone works together to break the ice. Even if the beginning feels forced, the team effort is usually enough to get the conversation flowing.

"Everyone Else is So Much More Confident!"

They're not. Firstly, while talking to an author friend during downtime at a convention in spring 2019, she referred to me as "quite charismatic." This compliment, though flattering, caught me by surprise because I always felt that I struggled with charisma.

In everyday life, I'm quiet and would never draw attention to myself at parties. I never liked performing. My hands sweat whenever I approach someone I deem important and I tend to overthink jokes I make to new acquaintances. I spend a lot of time in my own head and had previously assumed that showed in conversations. Obviously, that's not the case because, while I've been fretting and thinking everyone else has more confidence, so have my fellow authors. They've been so focused on their slipups that they haven't noticed mine.

I've known successful action/thriller author Steven Moore for three years. He brought to light a startling revelation on this topic in a Facebook post he wrote in 2018. We've eaten together, grabbed drinks at bars and spoken on social media. At events, he's always seen buying authors drinks and chatting passionately about adventures he's had while travelling. It was easy to think he had no social anxiety whatsoever.

It turns out he hides his struggles well. According to that Facebook post, he undergoes (suffers) a regimen of mental trials before conventions, much like a stage performer – shaking, nausea, pacing, often not making it out of the door at all. It's a complete contrast to the confident professional I know. Buying drinks for networking acquaintances, I later realised, is his crutch – a way to break the ice and feel less like he's inconveniencing other conference guests when he wants to talk to them.

It seems extreme but this inner struggle is more commonplace than you might expect. I have used the same drink-buying tactic and I know others have too. Sure, there are some extroverted networkers who thrive on hectic crowds and hundreds of voices speaking at once, but they are rare.

Keep a lookout for the crutches people use to boost their confidence. Some buy drinks, others ridicule big names, some tell edgy jokes they later regret, and many get drunk or only talk to one person at a time. Emotional armour comes in different forms. It's worth observing the room at an event to notice them. You can't always tell exactly what insecurity they are hiding but you can be sure of one thing: not everyone is as confident as they would like you to believe.

"Everyone Else is So Much Better!"

Commonly referred to as "imposter syndrome", this belief often afflicts corporate employees promoted before they feel they're ready to manage a team. However, it is also ubiquitous among writers. Simply put, it's the belief that you're not as good as your peers, don't deserve your success and that, one day, you will be found out. Instead of talking about it openly, many people cover up their insecurities with fake confidence.

For writers, imposter syndrome manifests as doubts in their own writing or marketing expertise. They don't see themselves as being great at either because they struggle to see past their own shortfalls. This is particularly present among self-published authors because they lack the validation of being chosen by a traditional publisher. Hence, they feel pressure to demonstrate extra abilities in the marketing and publishing processes to make up for not being told they're a great writer.

I mention this phenomenon because it's often unclear why any book becomes a success. Even decades-old traditional publishers haven't cracked the code. If they had, every title they released would be a bestseller and they'd never sign a dud. Yet, despite this truth, successful self-published authors are constantly quizzed for tips and strategies by audiences of hopeful writers. Not being able to answer these questions can cause these authors anxiety as they face the possibility that maybe they simply got lucky and couldn't repeat past victories.

Traditionally published authors, by contrast, can direct that question to their publisher who (hopefully) has a marketing plan. That frees them up to talk about writing great prose, comforted by the idea that their writing advice is sound because their publisher said they're good.

In both cases, the authors give advice while, at the same time, hoping they aren't asked anything that will expose their apparent shortfalls. The truth, however, is that neither author should be so hard on themselves. Their knowledge has grown over time without them noticing the mountains they've climbed. In reality, "imposters" are more capable than they think.

And, weirdly, imposter syndrome never stops, regardless of the scale or longevity of your success. On a panel at New York's

2018 ThrillerFest, a huge author conference, R. L. Stine, Lee Child, Clive Cussler and others talked about this issue at length. Between them, they'd hit the *New York Times* bestseller list dozens of time, won multiple awards, created household characters and sold over 600 million books. Yet, when asked about self-doubt, their answers were unanimous:

"Even after making the bestseller lists so many times, I feel like a fraud."

That line came from Sandra Brown who had, at the time, penned 36 *New York Times* bestselling romantic suspense novels. It was safe to say that she wasn't a fraud but that didn't stop her brain maintaining the lie. And the others felt the same. That's a good lesson to take away from some of the industry's most successful names: most people feel like frauds, so the best strategy is to accept that this feeling exists and keep working regardless.

There will be exceptions; there always are. Some writers are born with an unnerving amount of confidence. In some cases, they manage to back it up with near-superhuman talent. Other times, they are left baffled by the prospect that readers might not like their work.

Most people, though, experience bewilderment, overwhelm, imposter syndrome and insecurities. When you begin your authorial journey, everyone will seem more qualified, knowledgeable and talented than you – and that won't change. Thankfully, you can use that knowledge to stop yourself being daunted by bigger authors when networking. Be comforted by knowing that, while you're trying not to sound stupid, so are they.

"What if I'm Overbearing?"

Many writers worry about being shy but not everyone is the same. While some people act brash to overcompensate for their insecurities, others just naturally have a dramatic personality and don't even know it.

If you find yourself being a touch too loud, it's fine as long as you're self-aware and make an effort to curb the worst of your habit. As much as you might love expressing strong opinions and making yourself the focal point of conversations, to most people that's terrifying behaviour. It will intimidate quiet contacts and cause you to butt heads with potential collaborators.

We have all encountered those we deem over-the-top: arrogant, attention-seeking narcists, oblivious to the tension that follows them like a nebulous cloud.

Some people are too much and don't know it. Some are, and have suspected it for some time. As you're reading this chapter, you either worry needlessly or you're in the latter camp and are perfectly positioned to help yourself. Don't worry about it. Just be sure to calm yourself and allow those who are less confident an occasional opening to speak. That way, rather than disregarding you as a windbag, others will pay attention when you participate and be entertained by your confidence.

"What if They Don't Like Me?"

By her own admission, my good friend and fiction cover designer, Zoe Foster, doesn't attend networking events because she believes she doesn't make a good first impression. In her own words: "I'm very good at rubbing people up the wrong way." From my perspective this isn't true.

What she deems blunt and offensive, I call straight-talking and honest, two qualities I value. Her advice is constructive and she knows her subject. She just overthinks her conversations and worries about causing offence.

It's easy to link networking performance to self-image but this is one insecurity you must overcome to be an effective networker. Action will either allow you to grow or teach you a lesson – and both are good outcomes. Inaction when it comes to networking, on the other hand, will only ever keep you in limbo, safe but ultimately unfulfilled.

Not everyone will like you. That's true for everyone. They won't get your humour or agree with your views. Knowing this won't necessarily make a personal rejection any easier but it will give you the wisdom to try again elsewhere without being too hurt.

There are, however, two pieces of advice I can offer to make this process easier to stomach. The first is that some people *will* like you, no matter your personality. It's a numbers game, especially at events where lots of people share common interests, so you will always make a good impression on *someone* eventually.

The second piece of advice is that you can actively make yourself a more desirable contact. We addressed it in the context of online networking but it's equally applicable for real-world meetings.

Professionalism.

Being professional can instantly boost your likeability in a networking setting. You don't have to change your personality, just filter it to remove anything that will put people off.

One practical way you can do this is by avoiding controversial topics like abortion, religion or politics. Subjects like those spark healthy debates among friends but are best left at the door when talking to strangers. You never know what experiences they have and how they will react.

Likewise, don't go into depth about your success unless you're invited to prove your expertise, because it will usually come across as boastful. Humility and light conversation is a better approach.

Steering clear of edgy jokes unless you're confident they will land well is also a good practice. Being funny can make you stand out but, if you're not sure your present company will appreciate your humour, it's better to let the joke go unsaid.

You don't have to be the life and soul of the party and there's nothing wrong with simply being known as polite. A good rule of thumb is to remember that people like to laugh but they prefer to make other people laugh. So, one of the best things you can do is hold your tongue when it comes to controversial comments and laugh along to jokes said by others.

The point of this section isn't to strip you of your personality. It's to help you avoid saying things that might hinder your progress or later play on your mind. If you want to make a risky joke, read the room and go for it if you think it will be a hit. You don't want to scrub the colour out of your personality, but you might want to polish it so it's the best it can be.

Alternatively, if choosing your words carefully doesn't sit well with you, you could take a stronger stance and become a Marmite® personality who is loved by some but hated by others. That means standing up for what you believe in no matter the consequences. It's a bold tactic and is sure to polarise your acquaintances. Some will wince at your every word, but you will bond quickly and more strongly with those who share your views or respect your confidence.

While I don't do this myself, it's an equally viable option. It just harbours more risk. The one key benefit here, however, is that whether you're hated or loved, you will always be remembered.

"What If My Online Friends Don't Recognise Me?"

The people you encounter at physical meetings run by online communities often don't match the faces you see on social media. Some active members will be too busy to attend. Others look different to their profile pictures. Lurkers – those who read online posts but don't contribute – reveal themselves, preferring to get involved in person. A few attendees might not even be in the online group as they heard about the event elsewhere – perhaps the organiser's newsletter or a poster in a local library.

For those reasons, it's best to treat a physical networking event as a fresh crowd and expect to know nobody. It's important to remember, as unrecognisable as you think some people are in real life, it's possible they think the same about you. Don't panic, though. You can still turn a completely fresh face into a valuable contact without having to rely on existing rapport.

Having said that, it's rare not to recognise *anyone* at these events. One of the most common phrases uttered at them is, "I recognise you from your profile pic." If you've built up a trusted reputation online, you will almost certainly be told this by someone.

Your first encounter of this kind will be strange because your conversation partner might know you, but you might not have any knowledge of them. At other times, you will be vaguely familiar with each other but not know each other's name. It makes sense. We live in an industry of pen names and alter-egos so confusion is inevitable. The best way to handle this is to be polite and assume nobody knows anyone. Introduce yourself and ask the other person their name even if you think you know it. That way, nobody is left with a red face.

Even if a stranger calls you by your first name, introduce yourself in full anyway. People do make mistakes and that can lead to all kinds of embarrassment once you've realised too late in the conversation that you thought you were talking to someone else entirely.

As a good rule of etiquette, it's best to introduce yourself, regardless of whether you've met once before. I do this whenever I stumble upon a familiar face because I've engaged in confusing conversations first-hand. At one event, an author I see regularly appeared unexpectedly and greeted me with all the warmth of an old friend. It took me 15 minutes of name-dodging and surreptitiously glancing at his ID badge before I saw his name and the whole thing clicked. Out of context and not expecting to see him at that event, my mind drew a blank. It's easily done.

To help your existing acquaintances to avoid having to admit they don't remember your name, re-introduce yourself, saying something like:

"Hi, Sarah. Good to see you. Daniel Parsons. We met last year
at the Rhondda Book Fair."

Offering your name and where you last spoke instantly stops your contact from scrambling to place you. At the very least, it allows them to pretend to remember you and avoid embarrassment. If you forget to do this at the outset but realise the person has no idea who you are, you can save them by referring to yourself in third person or making an excuse to show them your book covers on your phone where they can read your name.

No need to worry if none of your online friends are attending an event, or if they don't recognise you. There are easy ways to avoid these social banana skins. Whether or not they know you to begin with doesn't really matter. What matters most is whether they think of you fondly by the end of the event.

"WHAT IF I GET OVERWHELMED?"

Everyone gets overwhelmed at events, particularly if they last several days in large venues. You're in an unfamiliar environment, surrounded by hundreds or thousands of people, advertising is everywhere and your senses can't process it all. Given an avalanche of choices, your brain filters out all but what's in front of you to survive. What usually ends up happening is that, after several hours, you get a headache, a sore throat, and what you really want to do is find someplace comfortable to sit and rest your feet. And there are *never* enough chairs!

Inevitably, this means you won't talk to *everyone* you planned to meet. The first time you visit an event, you might take lots of notes at seminars but not manage *any* meaningful conversations. But that's okay. Many reserved attendees do it every year, preferring to keep to themselves.

A reputation isn't built in a day. If this is your first conference, then getting overwhelmed and not capitalising on every opportunity is understandable. I've now attended The London Book Fair six times. When I arrive at Olympia, the venue that now hosts it every year, my day starts by grabbing a map from an information desk and heading straight for *Author HQ* where I give myself 30 minutes to drink iced coffee and read through my plan for the day to refresh my memory.

There, I usually bump into old friends, greet new faces and immediately get chatting. Typically, someone suggests we meet for lunch before I head off to my first seminar. It's a pleasant experience and one that I've come to take for granted. But my arrival didn't always look quite so organised.

Picture the scene: it's spring 2013. I set off from Cardiff at 4:00 am on a sombre coach and arrived after 9:00 am. I was sweaty, carting a backpack full of books, sandwiches and business cards, and had no idea what I was doing. Fumbling to get my ID badge scanned, I pushed my bag through the security check and wandered the Grand Hall for an hour, lost in a maze of stands.

It wasn't until I found another exit that I discovered the information desks. The staff gave me a map but, as I'm not a natural navigator, that didn't help. The venue contains two huge halls that look the same to the untrained eye. Within minutes of marching, I got more lost, missed my first two seminars, and ended up perched uneasily in Author HQ, slurping a ludicrously expensive smoothie.

That first year, I took some notes but spent most of my day struggling with the layout. Eventually, I got talking to some equally lost newbies and was invited to join them for drinks after the conference. Unfortunately, I couldn't go because, rather than investing in a hotel so I could freshen up and network the night away, I'd booked a return coach for that evening. I vowed not to repeat that mistake but had to wait 12 months to try again.

You see, there is a marked difference between my earliest and my most recent conference appearances. Now I go with a plan, knowing roughly who I want to meet and what I want to achieve. But that's only possible because I now have experience. Even with that advantage, I don't always tick every box on my agenda. Fluidity is key at these events because you never know what unexpected opportunity or complication will arise on the day.

If you're completely new to conferences full of advertising and social buzz, it's important to give yourself some slack. You won't become the most well-connected person in the building on your first visit. Most attendees never meet even a small percentage of visitors. All you can really do is set yourself reasonable expectations, such as talking to one speaker or meeting one other writer, and celebrate these small victories. Expect to get lost and tired, so stay hydrated and talk to at least one person you didn't know before that day.

"What If I Don't See My Ideal Contact?"

Realistically, you won't always get to chat to that one person you wanted to meet. Probability suggests that your number one dream meeting partner is an influencer. They probably run a successful business and reach thousands of followers every week, many of whom will be at the same event. At least within the bubble of the conference, they're famous. If you're intent on tracking them down, so are other visitors. These people are in high demand and will be locked in intimate conversations for the majority of the day. When they're not busy speaking on stage, they're caught in a swarm of admirers, or silently hiding in the toilet trying to decompress.

I've seen this first-hand as one of the jostling admirers. In 2015, I spotted an author and podcaster at a convention whose work I genuinely admired. If networking dream teams were a thing, she was certainly on mine. However, grabbing her attention for more than a few seconds was easier said than done. At first, I loitered, surreptitiously checking out stands and chatting to vendors while my target was engaged with another fan. The moment they left, I peeled away from a stand and weaved towards her. But before I got there, another visitor slid in from behind a carboard display and cut in front of me.

Taken aback, I wandered off for 10 minutes and circled back, hoping this second visitor had finished their conversation. However, when I returned and saw the conversation being wrapped up, it happened again. Another lurker stole my spot. It was only then that I noticed them. They were everywhere – authors, waiting, some more comedically than others, hidden behind newspapers or tying their shoes like cartoon sleuths.

All were playing it cool, pretending they hadn't noticed this industry rock star while at the same time hiding in plain sight. As I stood there, more passers-by noticed the special guest and almost tripped over themselves to change pace and creep closer. Meanwhile I quickly realised that my conversation would be awkward, clipped short by the pressure of the crowd waiting for their turn.

I decided not to stick around, opting instead to say hi, grab a quick fan selfie and move on so the next lurker could take my place. Fortunately, I later learned that this was a good decision. For a start, we wrote in different genres. Even if I were more established, our audiences didn't overlap so we couldn't help each other. Just because someone's famous, that doesn't automatically make them a good contact.

At the time, I didn't realise it, but I was better off making friends with authors and vendors more on my level. We had far more in common and were able to contribute value to the relationship and collaborations.

Later that day I did exactly that, forming an alliance with fellow fantasy and horror author Michael John Grist. Years later, we still share marketing ideas and support each other's launches, bringing value to each other.

You don't need to meet *everyone*. You can't. Many can't offer value, even idols you admire. In fact, you don't have to meet *any* of them, unless you've organised a meeting in advance. The beauty of large-scale networking events is that you never know who you're going to bump into, and sometimes the best encounters are those that happen by chance.

Actions to Take

To tackle the most common pre-event concerns:

- ✓ Anticipate mindset slips and learn to fight on regardless
- ✓ Condition yourself not to overthink everything you say and do
- ✓ Realise you're probably better at talking to strangers than you think, even if you're shy
- ✓ Know that many networkers struggle with social interactions too but they hide it well
- ✓ Accept that you might never outgrow imposter syndrome but don't let it stop you
- ✓ Check that you're not overbearing
- ✓ Ignore those who dislike you and focus on the people who want to share your circle
- ✓ Avoid controversy if you want to get on with everyone or embrace it if you want to deepen particular bonds
- ✓ Expect people to look different to their online profile
- ✓ Don't rely on being recognised
- ✓ Tell contacts who you are and how you know them to avoid confusion, even if you've met
- ✓ Cut yourself some slack if things don't go according to plan
- ✓ Don't expect to see results overnight
- ✓ Focus on realistic contacts over industry superstars because you'll have more to offer each other
- ✓ Build on small victories today to achieve greater opportunities tomorrow
- ✓ Know that sometimes the best encounters are the ones you don't expect

10

PREPARING FOR EVENTS

Mental preparation is important for networking success. However, you need to combine it with practical preparation to get the best results. In this chapter, we will explore what actionable steps you can take before an event to help you succeed. Some advice comes from personal experience, whereas other tips have come as recommendations from trusted, successful sources.

It's possible to feel your own way in the dark but these tactics will save time you would otherwise spend correcting mistakes. Whether you're completely fresh to networking, or an old hand, you will find something to boost your preparation game.

BOOK A HOTEL

If the event is far away and spread over more than one day, I can't stress this enough: book a hotel. Even if you *could* commute and attend without booking one, the advantages of having a room are too plentiful to ignore, if you can afford it.

The first time I visited The London Book Fair, I didn't follow this advice. To save money, I underwent an extremely early commute and spend the day struggling against an uncomfortable brain fog. Plus, I missed an author afterparty – a side-event where authors gather in a bar after the main conference closes for the day – because I had nowhere to stay the following night and had to return home for my day job.

Due to these mistakes, I only got a fraction of the worth out of my first big networking experience. In return for saving cash, I forfeited focus for the day, comfort, and the ability to attend an additional networking opportunity that night. Don't be like Young Dan. Companies book business class plane seats and comfortable hotel rooms for employees for a reason: employees who arrive at meetings well-rested perform better. You don't need to travel like a royal but there is definitely merit to be found in booking accommodation.

As a minimum requirement, for a multi-day networking event, you should book a hotel room for the night before the event so you can arrive well-rested. If possible, you should also add an additional night to take advantage of any extra invitations you receive during the day.

Visitors who live nearby are often eager to do extra networking after the official itinerary has ended as they don't have to worry about getting home. And those who are staying in a hotel have little else to do so will be keen to make the most of their short stay. That means people go out for drinks, meals, or see the sights together.

Join a Professional Organisation

Signing up to organisations like ALLi, the Scattered Author Society or the Society of Authors can provide worthwhile benefits. If you also help other writers to publish, the Independent Publishers Guild is an additional option, besides many more.

The main benefits of membership are usually on their website – like having access to experts who can talk you through publishing contracts to ensure you get a fair deal. One of the best perks is getting access to networking events for members. Sometimes you can tag along if you're not a member but you're unlikely to know when and where they are unless you call them or keep tabs on their website. Even then, they won't necessarily advertise *every* meeting because some will be invite-only.

Membership to these organisations gives you first-hand access to announcements. Even if they aren't hosting their own gathering, just having the organisers there means having a familiar contact you can talk to when you arrive at any venue where they have a presence.

The fact they're extremely busy, torn between entertaining existing members and shepherding potential new recruits, doesn't matter. In fact, it gives you an opportunity to show your worth and become a valued member. Being valued isn't something you can pay extra for; it's earned. I've seen several authors enter an organisation's trusted inner circle by helping in this way. It doesn't take a lot of effort. All you usually have to do is chat to interested newbies about the community and its benefits while the organiser is busy signing someone.

Authors I know who started this way have since gone on to be central figures in the community, invited to host podcasts and speak onstage for the organisation. The community's clout gave them social kudos, opportunities and confidence they would have struggled to achieve on their own.

FOLLOW GROUP ACTIVITIES AND TRENDING HASHTAGS

Advertising an event doesn't stop the moment the event starts as it once would have, and it doesn't always look like advertising. Gone are the days when event organisers went building to building, slapping posters on notice boards. There's still a place for billboards and ads printed in magazines for the bigger trade shows but many events aren't promoted with traditional adverts anymore.

Do you know how lots of conferences are now promoted? Influencers. People of influence with huge social media followings. They either create events of their own or they are asked to broadcast the news of events run by someone else. Not all shout-outs are paid ads but they are in some circumstances.

Having said that, organisers still need to use other tactics. Alongside spreading the word, they also create Facebook groups and hashtags for Twitter and Instagram. That way, ticket holders can talk to each other and share their experiences so people who aren't attending can follow the action.

Marketing in this way doesn't stop as soon as the doors open. It continues throughout the event and beyond. Attendees talk about how they got to the event, where they're staying, who they've met, the lessons they've learned, what they plan to do differently next year.

Much of this activity resembles native social media activity and blogging more than marketing carried out by the organisers. It's an example of what I refer to as complicit marketing – word of mouth, broadcast in the form of tweets, videos, images and soundbites. And it's all disguised as social commentary because those helping are customers who have become invested in the event and want it to succeed. They share selfies and write things like:

> "*En route* to #20BooksVegas! It's so good to have wi-fi again after such a long flight."

Or:

> "Met up with an old friend at The London Book Fair for pizza today. #LBF"

While organisers undoubtedly love free advertising, they aren't the only ones who profit. There are lots of side benefits that extend to those who can't go but still want to follow along, like live-streamed seminars and getting a sense of being there without having to travel. The biggest winners, though, are those attending the event.

One way they benefit is by scrolling through a group feed or a communal hashtag to identify their fellow attendees. In doing so, they can spot them anywhere and instantly fire up a conversation, providing they've done a little research. You can do this yourself to figure out who you want to meet, what interests them and where they are going to be.

I've personally used this tactic to pre-schedule meetings. It's a great time-saver as it allows you to line up meetings rather than rely on serendipitous encounters.

The final benefit of an event having a social media presence is that new-found friends can connect more easily afterwards.

You won't always remember a person's name after a chance encounter, but you'll probably be able to pick them out and befriend them if they're tagged in a photo that shows up in your feed.

MAKE CONTACT ONLINE AHEAD OF TIME

Professionals are open to accepting friend requests from complete strangers more than the average person. That receptiveness amplifies when both parties have mutual friends and they are attending the same event. Therefore, the weeks before an event is a great time to scroll through a list of attendees and shoot off requests to contacts that are more likely to be open to meeting.

This trick is especially true when it comes to big names. Successful, charismatic and in-demand, these people get plagued by more requests than they can manage. Accepting too many means risking turning their social media feeds into white noise. Therefore, they are selective. As someone who probably isn't yet a recognisable name, it's possible you won't make the cut.

Sending a friend request to these superstars close to the start of an event you're both about to attend changes things. For a start, by attending the same event, you're proving you're like them. Also, that the two of you share a mindset and have a lot in common. Plus, who wants to turn down a friend request from someone they're about to meet? It's awkward. As long as you make up for it by being a worthwhile contact, everyone wins.

If your request isn't accepted, don't worry. Some authors have never accepted a request I sent them years ago, despite us being on speaking terms. They still include me in projects so it's not like it damaged our relationship. Some people just prefer to separate their work and private lives. The key is not to bring it up. It will only make you look petty.

In most cases, those attending the same event will reciprocate. Make the most of the connections who *do* want to form a link rather than dwelling on those who don't.

WORK OUT YOUR ITINERARY

If you visit a large trade fair, you'll discover it comes with a boatload of seminar options. The London Book Fair is a three-day event, boasting talks on editing, translation, movie rights, audio production, digital streaming, printing methods, future tech and more. Each day, there are 20+ talks and panels, all with different speakers. You can learn a lot and meet extraordinary people. However, getting the best out of each event takes planning.

Events overlap and many are delivered from different stages spread across the site. That means you must plan your itinerary ahead of time.

A good way to get as much value as possible is to print out the entire multi-day itinerary – usually scores of potential talks – and whittle away the ones you don't mind missing. That leaves you with a list of four to five a day, consisting of must-visits and sessions that sound interesting. It's possible to fit in more but that would allow no wriggle-room to network in-between or navigate your way around the building.

You don't have to stick to this list. It's a guideline to keep you on track and stop you scrambling for a map while picking events on the fly. Planning will allow you to feel calmer and more prepared in an otherwise chaotic few days. In turn, that will give you the mental bandwidth needed to make great decisions and jump on opportunities that come your way.

PRACTICE YOUR ELEVATOR PITCH

Rambling is not a good quality in writing or a speech, but it's especially frowned upon in networking. Once you've been to a few events, you'll be able to spot the perpetrators. They're usually "that guy" people try to avoid. Never self-aware, they suck innocent bystanders into unending conversations, without getting to the point or providing value. Victims leave the conversation usually by making a polite excuse, pretending they've seen someone they've "been meaning to chat to all day" or dashing off to the toilet.

Don't be that person. It's easy to avoid. Just keep in mind these two things:

1. Everyone's time is valuable, including your own.
2. Your message must be clear.

Everyone's time is valuable. If people are attending a networking event, they want something out of it – knowledgeable friends, collaboration partners, marketing intel, whatever. To achieve these aims they need to meet enough acquaintances to find the right fit. That's how they establish who can deliver them the most value, unless they've done their homework and know exactly who they are looking for.

This isn't selfish. It's the whole point of being there. It's why you're there too, and why you don't want to spend all day talking to one person or forcing one person to spend their whole day talking to you.

That brings us to point two, your message. You need an elevator pitch to showcase what you are about in a short time. An elevator pitch is a short sales hook that presents the essence of a product or service (in this case you and your books) as fast as possible. Having one allows you to network more efficiently. Normally, it's one or two sentences – something you would say quickly to a potential contact during a short elevator journey. Hence the term elevator pitch.

I'll give my own as an example. The first time I visited an author afterparty, I had a few fantasy and horror books under my belt. My aim was to meet other authors who wrote in those genres so we could set up newsletter swaps. Thus, my elevator pitch was:

Hi, I'm Daniel Parsons. I write young adult fantasy and comedy horror books.

When my conversation partner probed further, I'd quickly release details like:

I've had 1,000 paid book sales and 40,000 free downloads.

Yeah, I've got a mailing list. It's up to about 10,000 members – 7,000 fantasy readers and 3,000 horror.

Notice how quickly these examples dispense key details? At first glance it seems robotic but that's exactly the information many new contacts want to know in these sorts of situations. Are you an author? A publisher? A distributor? If you are an author, what do you write? You need to be clear on your genre – none of this "it's complicated" nonsense. People switch off very quickly if you can't give them a clear idea of where your books sit.

Answering with anything other than a known genre comes across as amateurish. Remember, if you can't describe your book, publishers can't market it and authors won't know if their audience will like it.

Hard numbers come second. It's important not to lead with them because it can look like bragging. Normally, if nobody asks, I wouldn't share them but, if it seems like someone is testing to see if we're on the same level, stating raw numbers is the fastest way to find out.

The best-case scenario is you'll find someone on a similar level willing to work with you. Worst case, you'll be too small a fish to consider because you won't be able to provide enough value in return. However, at least in the latter case, you have proven that you know your numbers and haven't wasted anyone's time. If you find yourself in a situation where you are the big fish, the power is in your hands. Here, you will need to decide whether you can come up with some sort of relationship dynamic that is mutually beneficial, which is sometimes possible if the newbie has a lot of untapped potential that you can help them achieve.

The elevator pitch works, especially if you create one for yourself and one for each of your books. Distilling an 80,000-word novel into a two-line summary isn't easy but it can provide extra clarity and sell your books' unique selling points better than a long pitch.

Here is an example, this time from Suzanne Collins' *The Hunger Games*:

The Hunger Games is a young adult sci-fi novel about teenager Katniss Everdeen. When her younger sister is ordered by a dictator to enter a deadly combat tournament against teens from neighbouring districts, Katniss volunteers to take her place alongside a boy who has loved her since childhood.

You see, saying Collins is a sci-fi author doesn't really hit the nuances of her books' sub-genres – the romance and dystopian elements. Another sci-fi writer might be interested in running a newsletter swap with Collins. However, that wouldn't necessarily be the case if they knew they were agreeing to promote a romance-heavy story about a teenage heroine to their audience of gore-loving robot fanatics.

Being clear and specific upfront with your elevator pitch *will* put off some contacts, but that's fine. It stops you both wasting time and having to part ways awkwardly when the salient details finally emerge after thirty minutes. Those who like what you tell them, however, will be more interested because of your candid introduction. Plus, this encounter will allow you more time to work out strategies or to move on quickly so you can both make more friends.

PREPARE ANECDOTES

Preparing anecdotes isn't essential but it can be useful if you constantly find yourself bumbling into boring or inappropriate stories. You know the ones – funny at the bar, not so funny when you're trying to impress a publisher.

When it comes to being boring, you're probably not. It just seems that way if you look at the media. Celebrities are presented as treasure troves of hilarious anecdotes on talk shows. YouTube and Instagram are dominated by entrepreneurs who have six-pack abs, celebrity friends *and* a private jet. Everyone's more interesting than you. Or at least, that's what they would have you believe.

The truth is, celebrities on talk shows seem uncommonly entertaining but only because they have unfair advantages. Firstly, audiences eat up even the most mundane A-list story because they are already fans. It's easy to be interesting when everyone *wants* to hear you speak. Secondly, these stars are coached by PR professionals who tell them what to say and how to say it. Also, their interviews are edited in post-production. Awkward silences are removed and canned laughter is stuffed in. Celebrity appearances are products, just as polished as a novel.

Social media stars are the same. Notice how they're often surrounded by friends, looking glamourous, caught up in zany adventures? Vloggers are particularly guilty here, always pretending they have a fun experience ahead. The reality is that those filmed moments are staged snapshots, poised between long periods of normality.

That's why they always look less fun when fans run into them in the street. Dressed in a scruffy hoody, they're found wearing glasses you'd never see on their official content, armed with a supermarket shopping bag. It's because they're normal. They are just good at hiding their daily routine.

There's no need to consider yourself boring if you don't have a hundred adventures full of hijinks at your fingertips. You probably have more fun things to talk about than you realise.

Noting them down before going to a networking event takes the pressure off having to think on your feet.

A list of five should do and they can be anything from the ridiculous to the intriguing. There's no pressure to be funny or to flex your success. Being relatable and mildly amusing is enough. Here are some examples:

The time you got an interview at your dream university and it went so badly the professor started recommending other institutions.

That time you failed to do the worm in a dance-off because you didn't know you had to use your arms.

The fact that you went through a red light five minutes into your driving test then joked about learner drivers to your examiner.

The night you got interrogated by Hong Kong Airport customs officials because you damaged your passport.

How it felt to do a bungee jump.

The Route 66 road trip you did with your friends when you were 22.

These are all true stories from my life. Highlights. Not everyday occurrences. Not all of them show me in a good light, none of them name-drop a celebrity and few are funny. But they are interesting enough to fall back on if a conversation wilts.

Note down some for yourself and see how interesting you really are. You don't have to use them on the day. Shoehorning one into a conversation makes no sense and you'll probably find more natural ones as you start talking anyway. They're just there if you need them.

This tactic also helps those who find themselves hurtling into an obscene story and then having to backpedal. If you do this then it might also be worth writing down the anecdotes you probably shouldn't bring up in polite company, unless you're certain they will land well. Once you have your list, a quick re-cap before an event can ensure you have a library of conversation fodder.

DON'T SELL

We've covered this for online networking but it's worth revisiting for physical events. You must remember that you're not there to sell anything. Your aim shouldn't be signing people up to a course or product – not in the first meeting. That's not why these events run at all. If anything, doing so will only annoy the other guests and step on the organisers' toes.

As far as you're concerned, your only job at a networking event is to sell *yourself*. If you do that well, business will come your way in the long term. Be dazzling. Be erudite. Be witty. But don't be a sleazy salesperson.

There's nothing wrong with swapping details and having an elevator pitch to summarise what you do. The danger approaches when you take that elevator pitch too far and try to pressure people into making a financial commitment the moment you meet them. That's selling, not relationship building.

Have Business Cards

It's important to get business cards printed before your first event. They don't need to be fancy or expensive. Plain black text on a white background is fine as long as they contain the necessary information:

Your Name
Phone Number (Optional)
Email Address
Your Job (Author, Illustrator, etc.)
Website URL
Social Media Links or Handles

You can include other details if you have something special to share. For example, some people include their address. Others have double-sided cards if they have two jobs (e.g. author and editor).

Even if the card has a plain design, it reminds people that they met you and gives them the information they need to contact you again. Plus, it offers them your name which – take it from me – most people will have forgotten the moment you tell them, never mind days, weeks or months after the event.

Understand Your Options

You won't always feel powerful in a networking situation, surrounded by industry titans, but educating yourself and building a strong team of advisors can help you act more confidently. The publishing industry has always been a minefield for new authors. Contracts, for example, often cause tension because many authors don't know what rights they're signing away when they first begin. These can include:

- o Signing away worldwide rights despite a publisher only exploiting them in one country
- o Being paid only 8-12% of RRP on a book sale
- o Not being allowed to publish elsewhere until a whole series has been published, which could take years
- o Forfeiting the rights to a universe you created so you can only publish stories set in it with one publisher
- o Unknowingly signing away screen rights, seeing your work adapted and getting no extra income

While these terms might seem predatory, they're pretty common, and not necessarily because of publisher greed. Sometimes, new publishers make mistakes, taking more rights than they need because they don't know what they're doing and copy competitors' contracts. It happens. Authors aren't the only ones who learn as they go.

Margaret Attwood famously signed away her TV rights for *The Handmaid's Tale* and saw no royalties from the screen adaptation created by Netflix years later. The exposure boosted her book royalties but they tallied to a fraction of what she would have earned had she not signed away those TV rights.

If creatives did that today, it would be considered an even bigger mistake. This is because we are living in the "maker movement", a period that will go down in history as a golden era of DIY creativity. Thanks to the internet, artists from a variety of disciplines can now exploit their intellectual property and bring it to market.

Authors can publish ebooks on hundreds of online stores, print paperbacks with no upfront costs and sell to billions of smartphone users. They can record their own audiobooks, broker deals with studios and stream them to over 200 countries. They can sell their own translation rights or choose to translate them personally. Although it's not recommended in most cases, they can also negotiate their own movie deals with Hollywood. Every right you retain is one that can be exploited elsewhere to fill in the gaps missed by publishers.

There are lots of possibilities but being able to tease apart and exploit these rights requires a ton of research. Each decision is a potential banana skin. Even having a slightly-less-than-watertight contract with another author can mean the difference between riding high or being taken for a ride.

I'm not giving legal advice, but I do suggest building your network with this in mind. Lawyers and accountants are treasure-troves of information – the more specialised the better. Getting trusted advisors on your team in addition to learning yourself is the best approach.

Intellectual property law, foreign tax systems, mailing lists, formatting jargon, and so much more; you don't need to know every detail of these topics but educating yourself and surrounding yourself with those who do will prevent you from making mistakes.

When it comes to your options, there is often more than one right answer. Lots of traditionally published authors underestimate the potential of self-publishing but the opposite is also true. With thousands learning to self-publish every month, many writers completely overlook the benefits of traditional publishing deals. They're so caught up in the indie movement, they don't see how going "trad" could be their best option. How a deal could better suit their lifestyle goals. For this reason, I recommend knowing your subject but also keeping your mind open to alternative viewpoints as you learn.

BUILD YOUR TEAM

Billionaires often talk about diversification when they're asked for investing advice. Once they make their fortune, they quickly learn that the way to ensure they don't fall back to Earth is to diversify. That way, no matter what happens, they always have a portion of their cash invested somewhere that delivers returns.

In many ways, networking follows the same principle of diversification. The best way to network is to build a diverse, self-sufficient team of collaborators. They won't necessarily work together, but they will all work with you. And while one connection might propel you into the cosmos, it's important to maintain contact with alternatives. That way, if that stellar contact disappears, you still have the means to produce and market your own work.

That's why indie authors are often uneasy with the traditional publishing model. They know that, in that arena, writers are sometimes completely locked out of the fold. They hold little knowledge or access to the full team of professionals that work on their books unless they are already a household name. The publisher handles everything and can take it all away.

Admittedly, that's not the case with all publishers. Many independent presses and larger players that are keen on collaborating with their authors do introduce them to their in-house team. In-house publicists can even get their authors' feet in the door with prime media contacts. Additionally, agents can help nurture great relationships between writers and merchandisers. It's just not always the case because, like authors, traditional publishing professionals have to protect their own interests first. This *can* mean not giving away all of their secrets to authors who might prefer to cut them out of the process.

It's thrilling to be "picked up" by a decision maker but a more stable plan is to *become* that decision maker. To pick yourself. Building a team of savvy professionals to handle everything from your cover design to accounting is a lot more work but it means never finding yourself in a weak position. Never begging for exposure or someone else's business infrastructure to keep you growing.

Regardless of what method you use to publish your books, having a Plan B is logical. Building your own team that can help you bring books to market provides that safety net.

Visit Unfamiliar Exhibitors

At any conference where entrepreneurs congregate, service companies follow. This phenomenon is evident at almost every big publishing conference. The regulars are easily recognisable, especially if you're not a complete beginner: Penguin Random House and HarperCollins are examples of companies that work hard to remain a fixture on the publishing landscape.

But while they occupy the biggest stands, they can't necessarily provide the most value to your author business. That's because these companies are large enough not to care about a single author. It's hard to broker a deal with such juggernauts unless you're pulling in serious sales figures or have huge social sway. Half a million book sales and a "USA Today bestseller" title: that's the sort of bait you need to get the big fish to bite.

There's no need to look glum if you don't fit those requirements. Lots of opportunities can be found with smaller, less familiar companies. It's common knowledge, for example, that you can get your books printed with Amazon – a company so big they're unlikely to negotiate on unit price. However, did you know there are smaller printers that will haggle to get your business?

In the same way, a lot of up-and-coming online bookselling apps want to gain market traction. They don't have millions of customers but many have thousands. Offer to direct readers their way and they might be willing to feature your new release on their home page. Doing so would make you one of their highest-performing authors – a big fish in a small pond. It won't gain you worldwide clout, but that income trickle could grow into a torrent as the company expands.

You won't recognise these vendors but that doesn't necessarily mean they lack the ability to provide value. Two years ago, I was at a conference full of these service companies. One of the vendors was tiny, tucked away in a corner of the hall. The rep, a young man slouched in a foldup chair, was surrounded by posters in Mandarin Chinese. I approached and asked him what he represented.

"China Literature," he said, in a thick, Chinese accent, looking up from his smartphone.

I was astounded. China Literature isn't a big brand in the UK – or anywhere in the western world. However, it's arguably the biggest ebook retailer in China. Yet, they had a tiny one-man stand in London. A presence the majority of the event's attendees would never notice.

The rep walked me through his brochures while explaining that few authors ever approach him, even though China Literature had a self-publishing portal. This was a market that, while hampered by a rigorous government filtering process, was a potential diamond mine that went largely ignored. After thanking him for his time, I took the rep's business card and pamphlets, thrilled by the potential I had uncovered. Since then, I have found easier ways to reach the same market through the company Publish Drive but it's always good to have more options once you start to gain traction.

This sort of encounter isn't an isolated event. This is why it's worth visiting unfamiliar exhibitors. You never know what connections you'll stumble upon that the majority miss.

ACT POWERFULLY

According to an article published by *Ivy Exec*, a website that teaches elite professionals how to advance their careers:

"In business, knowing when to walk away is key – whether it means deciding against an acquisition that on paper would create significant synergies, saying no to a deal when the price is becoming unreasonable, leaving a toxic workplace, or simply leaving for a better atmosphere."

This advice applies to networking authors. That's because many self-identify as a "starving artist." As such, they go into conversations looking for someone to save them because they don't consider themselves to be business-minded. From their first word, they exude weakness that can almost always be overcome if they committed to understanding the *business* of publishing.

Some people experience genuine issues such as anxiety and dyslexia that limit their performance potential in business. However, the idea that starving writers are too "artsy" to learn basic business principles is often misinformed. Once you realise you can *choose* to save yourself, you can take on this well-informed Ivy Exec advice.

Negotiation success is dependent on power. If you go into every negotiation believing that you *need* a deal no matter the cost, your contact will sense that desperation and take advantage. That's how you end up with the brunt of a collaboration workload, your name printed smaller than someone else's on a book cover or a smaller cut of the profits.

By contrast, entering a conversation having decided that you don't *need* a particular outcome means opening yourself up to:

1. better terms because you're less likely to cave
2. contacts who respect you and your work

A powerful mindset can even mean getting a deal you once would have lost. The fact is, desperation isn't attractive. It comes across as weak and/or salesy. Lacking desperation and being prepared to part ways without a deal on the other hand, can make you warmer and more relaxed. Many creatives would rather work with that person because they hate hyper-competitive corporate personalities.

Ultimately, feeling you can walk away means potentially giving up a toxic "opportunity" now for an exciting one later. It makes negotiating more enjoyable. To make this easier, think of the whole experience as if it were a job interview. Only, you're not the interviewee, desperate for the job: you're the employer, assessing whether this stranger is right for your business. Thinking this way will help you make better decisions and lead you to work with people on terms that are mutually beneficial.

ENJOY YOURSELF

As a final tactic for your first event, my best advice would be to enjoy yourself. Relax! I mean, you're an author, hanging out with other people who love books. For some, that's living the dream!

Remember not to take this whole thing too seriously or you risk losing sight of why you started writing in the first place: because you love it. This event isn't some forced-fun occasion set up by your boss. It's an opportunity to talk to your friends and idols about stuff you both love and possibly to take your work to a whole new level. Love every minute.

Actions to Take

To prepare for your first event:

- ✓ Book a hotel for the night before so you can arrive fresh
- ✓ Consider joining a professional organisation so you know about afterparties and their organisers
- ✓ Follow online group activities and event hashtags to gauge who will be attending
- ✓ Pre-contact people you'd like to meet so you can schedule meetings
- ✓ Practice your elevator pitch
- ✓ Prepare a list of anecdotes if you're afraid of coming across as boring or overly controversial
- ✓ Don't prepare a sales pitch because nobody wants to be sold to at a networking event
- ✓ Order business cards to make it easier for people to remember your name and find you after the event
- ✓ Educate yourself and build a team of advisors to protect yourself from being misled
- ✓ Build a team to weatherproof your business from the loss of vital connections
- ✓ Visit unfamiliar exhibitors and ask questions to discover unexpected opportunities
- ✓ Act with a powerful mindset, not a desperate one
- ✓ Enjoy yourself because this is your dream

11

ATTENDING DAYTIME EVENTS

You've printed your ticket, organised transport and booked a hotel. You've adjusted your mindset, spoken to other attendees and organised meetings in advance. You're ready.

Now what?

Ticket in hand, you've still got no concrete plan of exactly how the day will go. Luckily, this chapter contains a foolproof, flexible strategy for getting the most out of a daytime event.

Here's a preview you can refence quickly once you are more accustomed with the steps:

1. Take a wingman.
2. Get there early.
3. Find your bearings.
4. Embrace detours.
5. Split up to cover more ground.
6. Shake your early nervous energy.
7. Visit talks.

8. Talk to speakers.
9. Give and request business cards.
10. Make yourself a social media beacon.
11. Say if you don't know something.
12. Be honest about your success.
13. Grab selfies with industry icons.
14. Network while you eat.
15. Show genuine interest in others.
16. Accept media opportunities.
17. Ask about additional events.
18. Invite new friends to additional events.

That might sound like a lot to take in but don't worry. Addressing these points will become second nature as you become more experienced. In the meantime, each subheading in this section addresses a different step, which should clear up any sticking points.

Whether you're a complete newbie or a returning veteran, the following ideas should help you not only survive but thrive in any hectic conference.

TAKE A WINGMAN

A wingman can be a fantastic social crutch for a new author finding their voice in a fresh networking arena. I've seen them come in many forms, from siblings and spouses to business partners and author friends. I have carpooled with my editor, split up at certain events, then regrouped over a meal to share highlights of what we've learned.

You don't *need* a wingman. In many cases, I've gone alone and done extremely well. So long as you're friendly and confident enough to approach strangers, you'll be fine. Just know that it's a viable option if you feel you need a little help getting started.

Get There Early

Arriving "fashionably late" isn't encouraged if you are booked to fill a table or speak onstage at a networking event. Nobody likes an empty seat or a late speaker. Visitors paid for a full venue and itinerary, so forcing an organiser to apologise for gaps will almost certainly mean having your slot rejected the following year.

If you go as a paying visitor, purely to network, you can turn up whenever you want but it's still worth turning up early. This enables you to put in some extra networking graft. The following strategy works better at smaller events, but it can help at larger ones too if you're allowed in the building early enough.

This is how it goes: inevitably, some authors with stands arrive late. Tables need to be moved, signs need to be fastened to posts and there are never enough hands to fix the mess before the masses flood the hall.

Lending a hand can gain you valuable brownie points with an event's key decision makers. These guys know everyone. That means, your help could earn you preferential perks, VIP access, or even private introductions to speakers.

Find Your Bearings

You'll want to scout out the site the moment you arrive. If the event is held at a small venue, grasping the layout shouldn't be a problem. However, navigating larger events can be mindboggling to a new visitor, even with attendants to offer directions. Grabbing a floor plan (if they offer one) and pinpointing landmarks on day one may seem like a waste of time but it will save you hours by not getting lost later on. Circling the whole venue will also give you an opening to approach vendors and organise meetings before their best slots are taken.

EMBRACE DETOURS

In an earlier chapter, we touched upon the importance of planning your itinerary. It gives your day structure and certainty, ensuring you squeeze every drop of value from an event. Regardless of whether you talk to a single person, it guarantees you see some great speakers, take detailed notes, and come away more informed than when you arrived. However, allow me to contradict myself briefly and make a case for ignoring it.

Event venues are often huge and mysterious. Potential lurks around every corner but so do wrong turns. Upon arrival, you might discover that two back-to-back talks you planned to attend are at opposite ends of the site. Getting between them involves unforeseeable challenges and, even if you ran, you'd arrive a sweaty, late mess. As well-meaning as your itinerary might have been, not every box will get ticked in practice.

But that doesn't matter. Here's why: between the two talks you recognise a big author wandering the stands. What are the odds! You would have missed them had the talks been next to each other, and meeting this person holds more networking potential than any presentation.

Plans get derailed but often a detour turns out to be a better route. Remember this when it happens because it's easy to let serendipity slip under the radar when you're too busy trying to stick to a less-than-ideal plan.

Split Up to Cover More Ground

If you've come with someone else, you'll probably have different agendas. Don't let the urge to stick together hold you back. Once you've become comfortable with this strange, new environment, part ways.

If your itineraries overlap, you should consider tweaking one to cover more ground. That way, as a pair, you can absorb more information and meet more people, then introduce each other to your new contacts.

Splitting up will also allow you to benefit from being a lone explorer. If you're alone you don't have a conversation buddy to rely on while standing in a line or waiting for speakers to talk. Two people working together can close off a conversation and appear unapproachable. A loner, on the other hand, is easier to approach, from a stranger's perspective, and more likely to start small-talk.

Shake Your Early Nervous Energy

Unless you're a practiced veteran or exude natural confidence, you'll probably enter the event carrying some nervous energy. You'll be conscious of how lost you look, and reluctant to strike up awkward conversations. Both problems are easily resolved.

The best way to avoid shutting yourself off is to deliver a quick punch of shock therapy. Find someone friendly, walk directly up to them and greet them with a smile. Don't overthink it. The more you loiter and dwell on what you're about to say, the more likely you are to flub your introduction.

I've held back for too long on many occasions. One time, I spotted an author I admire. It went as well as expected, given my inexperience. I gushed over the author for a few minutes, practically choked on my tongue, then sped away. Another time was under the snooty gaze of a rep for a high-profile company. I crashed and burned when it became clear that the rep looked down on self-published writers.

You know what, though? I don't regret either encounter. Both helped me get over my initial anxiety and, consequently, stopped me thinking about the worst-case scenario because it had already happened. After that, I relaxed because I knew the day could only improve.

These initial interactions might not be your best. However, if your contact is friendly enough to hold a conversation while you compose yourself, you'll improve. And if they're icy from the moment you start a conversation, don't worry about it. You were unlikely to charm them anyway.

Either outcome is fine. The purpose of these early interactions isn't to ignite a life-changing relationship. It's to flush your nervous energy and stop you worrying about your handshake and opening line while your heart races. Once that's gone, you can start talking more naturally to people who won't seem as big a deal but will probably be better connections in the long term.

Visit Talks

Conferences run talks on many subjects related to publishing. Mostly conducted by experts, or by panels of experts, the majority discuss concepts at entry level so any industry newcomer can listen without needing to Google every other word. However, this isn't *always* the case, particularly if you start networking at conferences aimed at savvy, experienced publishers, like NINC in Florida.

Regardless of your experience, you'll probably learn something new at these gigs. Speakers are information goldmines. So are other attendees. You can learn a lot simply by chatting to those sitting next to you in the crowd.

If you think logically, it makes sense. These people share your interests so they probably know something or someone who can help you. Audiobook talks, for example, are geared towards authors but they attract narrators and producers too. These people are primed to help you and love what they do. As long as you drop them a few knowledge bombs in return, everyone parts happily.

Talk to the Speakers

Speakers are knowledgeable and well-connected so not talking to them after an event has finished is a missed opportunity. Usually, this will mean having to hang around and wait your turn as spectators swarm the stage but the fruits you can reap from such conversations are potentially precious.

If kindling relationships is your goal, then this is a good place to do it. You know their field of expertise because you've just heard them talk and you no doubt have at least one burning question. Once they've answered it, be sure to request their business card and ask if you can send them follow-up questions. Often, they are happy to oblige. In fact, it's part of their networking strategy.

A secondary objective you have might be to become a speaker yourself. After all, look at the sense of authority it imparts. How the audience drinks in their every word and craves a slice of their time.

You'll still want to start by asking them a question relevant to the talk, otherwise you look self-interested. Though, you can follow it up by asking how they came to be a speaker at such a prestigious event. In some cases, they will offer to send you the organiser's contact details. Or they can point you to that person in the room.

After you've asked a question, always thank them for their time and keep their card. This type of contact can help you in more ways if you figure out what they struggle with and help them in return.

GIVE AND REQUEST BUSINESS CARDS

Remember those business cards you had printed for the occasion? Well, don't leave them in your hotel room! As a rough guideline, you should hand out as many as you take. That way, anyone who is interested enough in you to give you a card can look up your name and find out exactly what you do. So much of networking comes down to being known and this is one way to ensure that happens.

Make Yourself a Social Media Beacon

Let's start with a caveat. This tactic is controversial. For a start, I wouldn't recommend it if you're afraid of being vulnerable at an event in the first place. Having said that, it can work well if you have an active social media presence and you're not afraid of running into the odd weirdo.

The idea goes as follows: you broadcast a message on social media, letting people know that you're going to be near a landmark at a certain time, wearing certain clothes. Including the event hashtag or posting your message in a relevant group will enable other attendees to find you. Then all that's left to do is invite them to say hello.

I've seen several creatives try this, from authors to YouTubers. It is possible that nobody will turn up. However, the more well-known you are, the more attention you attract. Even as a newbie, though, you can attract fellow beginners, eager to snag their first contact. At any rate, it's worth a try, particularly if you want to make the most of a gap in your schedule.

Say if You Don't Know Something

There's a tendency to feel like you should know everything at these events. Everyone else seems to know the speakers, what they do and the jargon they use. It is wrong, however, to fake it if you don't understand a term.

You won't seem like an idiot if you simply state that you don't know something. In fact, your honesty will be appreciated. In these situations, everyone *loves* their subject, so there is always someone on hand to give you the lowdown on acronyms, tactics and people. Allowing them to explain will enrich your conversation. They'll get an ego-boost, you'll get an education and when it's over you will be in a better position to help answer the questions of others.

If you don't know something, someone else might not know either. They will be thankful you asked and cleared up their confusion so they didn't have to draw attention to their limited knowledge.

Don't worry about looking clueless or vulnerable. If everyone knew everything, why bother having speakers at all?

BE HONEST ABOUT YOUR SUCCESS

As with knowledge, it's tempting at these events to exaggerate your success. Doing so, though, will only disappoint your contacts down the road, which is worse than setting their expectations low in the first place. Are you completely new and unpublished? Let them know. Those further along in their career will impart more useful advice if they know your true position.

Are you an established author working part-time to make ends meet? Great! Many people at these events can relate. You see a lot of success stories online – those making five or even six figures a month – and it's understandable why this happens. Those mega-authors are killing it and their success is viral fodder. But lots more authors are quietly struggling with a day job. They'll relate more to people in the same boat.

Likewise, if you've already hit an uncommon level of success, tell people. You won't be seen as boastful as long as you have a good reason for saying it. If you're trying to drive home the relevance of your advice or pitching to a prominent potential collaborator, it's actually encouraged. Where you are on the career ladder doesn't matter because, at every level, your perspective gives you insights that are valuable to someone.

GRAB SELFIES WITH INDUSTRY ICONS

Selfies have replaced autographs and, in networking, that change has provided welcomed opportunities. Indeed, the value isn't in the selfies themselves but in sharing them. By tagging influencers you met (writing their name or handle so they get a notification) in your social media posts, you remind them about your conversation while promoting to your network that you have serious connections.

No matter how tenuous your link, the only message your followers will take from such an image is that you hang out with industry powerhouses. Therefore, it tells them you have the ability to reach influencers and that can make you a more attractive prospect. All from a simple photo.

Network While You Eat

Eating can be awkward during conferences if you don't know anyone. Many people opt to sit alone but it doesn't have to be that way. In fact, going for lunch can work in your favour as a friendship-building strategy because it enables you to talk without the pressure of a formal setting.

There are two ways to engineer a working lunch. One is to look for familiar faces who are already eating and ask to join them. This approach seems intrusive but it's generally appreciated. The relief of not having to sit alone can accelerate the bonding process and inspire others to approach if they see you succeed.

The second method is to invite someone to eat with you. The recipient won't always accept the invitation but it can work well. On occasion, you will even manage to get one-to-one time with a big name.

Show Genuine Interest in Others

As the day progresses, you'll shake lots of hands and talk until your throat burns. And while it's tempting to clock off the moment you think you've drunk the well dry, consider sticking around to help others. That's because, while you made connections, that's not necessarily true for your peers. Why not introduce two acquaintances if you think they have a lot to offer one another?

Showing genuine interest in other people's lives can make a huge difference to the depth of your relationships. You don't *have* to go this far to show you care, and people know that. As a result, it goes a long way in cementing you in both parties' minds.

Smiling is key. So is giving people your undivided attention. That means putting away your phone or laptop unless you're showing them something relevant to the conversation. Leaning in also shows that you're listening carefully to everything they are saying. If you follow up with appropriate questions or advice, your generosity will be remembered.

Accept Media Opportunities

With bright colours, social buzz and access to industry celebrities, publishing conferences are dream venues for media content creators. That's why companies and influencers are found everywhere during the day, firing up their cameras. Their audiences are hungry and these events are all-you-can-eat buffets.

If you're comfortable being recorded, this frenzy can provide fantastic ways to reach more readers and – you guessed it – contacts. What you get asked to do won't always be in your comfort zone but the requests are always interesting, beneficial and sometimes bizarre.

Personally, I've been asked self-publishing advice on camera for a university's e-magazine. I've appeared on a podcast recorded live in a bustling hall. I've been taken to a hotel room to record a testimonial. I was even invited to be an extra in a commercial (and then rightly cut out when the director discovered I couldn't act). It's fun! And the more opportunities you take, the more you're considered for others in the future.

Ask About Additional Events

If you've joined a professional organisation in advance, you'll probably already know if they are hosting an afterparty, business breakfast or other event for their members to mingle. However, theirs won't usually be your only option. Upon chatting to other attendees, you'll usually uncover more choices, including rival parties and group meals.

Learning about these events won't gain you automatic access but it could lead to an invitation. If you're asked to multiple get-togethers, you can even line them up and pack more value into conversations, knowing you will soon be gone so have to be economical with your time.

Invite New Friends to Additional Events

Once you know which extra events are available and weigh up your options, you will want to encourage other conference attendees to come with you. Of course, it's important to check with the organiser that the side-event isn't invitation-only first. But once you know anyone can attend, this is a great way to make more friends.

The friends or acquaintances you invite will be flattered and grateful that you thought to include them. Plus, the organiser will be pleased that you're helping them grow their networking side-event by attracting more people.

ACTIONS TO TAKE

On day one of a networking event:

- ✓ Take a wingman if you feel uncomfortable going alone
- ✓ Get there early and help the organiser, if possible
- ✓ Grab a floor plan and find your bearings
- ✓ Embrace interruptions and be open to tweak your itinerary
- ✓ Split up from your wingman to cover more ground
- ✓ Introduce yourself to a stranger to get rid of your initial nervous energy
- ✓ Talk to speakers and other visitors
- ✓ Give business cards to everyone you meet and request them
- ✓ Consider making yourself a social media beacon
- ✓ Admit if you don't know something so you and others can benefit from an explanation
- ✓ Be honest about your success because you'll have more relevant conversations as a result
- ✓ Grab and post selfies with industry icons to increase your perceived value as a contact
- ✓ Eat lunch with other visitors to build rapport at a time when they are more relaxed
- ✓ Smile, lean forward, ask questions, connect other people and give great advice to show that you care
- ✓ Accept all media opportunities that come your way
- ✓ Ask fellow attendees about extra events to give yourself more options
- ✓ Invite new friends to events you're attending to help them network and support the organiser

12
ATTENDING AFTERPARTIES

For the purpose of this book, we're going to call any side event that comes in addition to the main conference an afterparty. As such, the lessons in this chapter are applicable to actual parties but can also apply to small or large assemblies in hotel bars, group meals at restaurants, coffee mornings or business breakfasts set up for members who don't want to drink alcohol.

Whatever your personality or age, these are always inclusive events attended by authors and other professionals from all backgrounds. There's no need to limit yourself to lunches if you're a grandmother who writes cozy mysteries. Nor is the bar the only place to go if you're a 20-something graduate who only writes comedy thrillers and you think you would be out-of-place at a high-brow brunch. Attending a variety of afterparties will yield the best results because it will open you up to the widest range of opportunities.

Don't worry if that sounds daunting. As always, we will chunk this process into logical steps to ensure you maximise the networking value you receive.

FRESHEN UP

Unless schedules are tight, there will usually be a gap between the main conference wrapping up and the afterparties beginning. In some cases, this will be thirty minutes, in others, it can be as much as two hours. This is your opportunity to decompress and freshen up.

If you've booked a hotel nearby, you should use that resource to its full potential. Swing back to your room, clean your teeth, get changed and ensure you are party ready. If you haven't had food and aren't expecting any at the afterparty, you will also want to grab something on the way. These things tend to run late, sometimes stretching into the early hours. In that case, you don't want to be chatting (or drinking) on an empty stomach.

Gatherings like this tend to be smart-casual but the dress code really depends on your role. Publishing executives mainly come in suits, service providers in shirts and dresses, and authors turn up in whatever they want. There aren't any specific rules. Many authors started writing because they hated the rat race and wanted to stop wearing a tie. Therefore, nobody will judge a casual jeans-and-tee-shirt combination if that's what you want to wear.

The best practice is to make sure you're fresh and wearing something that makes you feel confident.

BRING THE PARTY

Afterparties are networking events but they don't carry the same formality as the official daytime ones. There are no talks, generally no structure and no requirements that mean you need to stick to business-only conversations. These functions are seen as celebrations, where authors and others have a chance to let loose. You will often find a free bar and guests like to make the most of it.

If you were wearing a tie early in the day, you can almost certainly leave it back at the hotel or tucked in your bag. Take business cards, of course, but don't go in with the expectation that the night will entirely consist of talking shop.

Facts, figures, agendas and professionalism should always be kept in mind but shouldn't dictate your experience. For many writers who don't work a nine-to-five, these parties are their equivalent of an office night out. And, like any good party, some members get a little looser than others. You don't want to end up throwing up outside while another author holds back your hair but there's nothing wrong with getting a little merry.

If possible, try to tread the fine line between wild celebration and professional poise. Bring business cards because you'll want your newfound buddies to find you after their hangover has faded, but don't stick to being professional. Strive for more personal connections because afterparties are where they thrive, usually helped along by tequila shots and a few hilarious antics. So, bring the cheer, bring the anecdotes and bring the energy. Most importantly, bring the party!

Find the Organiser

Upon arrival, the first person you should aim to find is the party organiser. You'll want to introduce yourself if you've never met, or re-introduce yourself if it's been a while since your last encounter. They see a lot of faces so it's always a good idea to jog their memory.

Usually, a benefit of meeting the organisers is that they indicate pretty quickly whether the bar is free. Thank them if it is. If not, offer to buy them a drink for putting on such a great event.

Given the nature of their position, they are typically the most well-connected person in the room and can introduce you to almost everyone. Seeking them out first is a life hack that has saved me time on multiple occasions and helped me to get into conversations with some of publishing's most interesting figures.

Circle the Room

Circling the room is a networking phrase that simply means moving frequently between conversations to meet a range of people. You don't have to meet *everyone*, just three or four interesting individuals to widen your horizons. An effective way to make sure this happens is to prepare a roster of polite phrases you can use to keep moving. Mine include:

Excuse me. I've seen someone I've been meaning to talk to all day.

Have you met Ted? I think you have a lot to offer each other. Catch you later.

I'm off to the bar to get another drink. Enjoy your night.

Because you're networking, and everyone wants the same thing, you don't need to feel guilty. Even if you're enjoying the conversation, sometimes it's necessary to keep moving. It's even acceptable to be explicit and say:

Oh, look, there's Julia I mentioned earlier. I hope you don't mind, I'm going to schmooze while I have the chance. Wish me luck!

At most events, everyone will understand your meaning. Having the confidence to break off a conversation in a polite manner during a lull means not wasting everyone's time, including your own. That way, you can meet more people, extend your influence faster and make the most of the event.

MEET YOUR ONLINE TRIBE

If you're an active member of a thriving online community, you tend to end up working with a lot of other members. Half of my team are ex-colleagues from the traditional publishing industry. However, I have worked with an editor, cover designer and a horde of marketing and distribution folk I've never met in the real world.

Conferences attract a lot of these familiar faces so they're great places to meet them. If any of your online team are attending, now is a good time to get to know the real people behind the emails and deepen your working relationship.

If you're just starting your career and you haven't published a book yet, then this sort of meetup can be even more beneficial. It can lead to an introduction with some of the industry's key designers and editors. Once you know them, you can also gather a consensus of their abilities and weaknesses from their clients in the same room.

Avoid a Wallflower Mentality

When eager creatives gather in a bar, it can be easy to turn away for a moment and find yourself locked out of conversations. Everyone is constantly getting distracted but there's no need to loiter awkwardly while you wait for an opening. Breaking into an existing discussion might seem daunting but you can do it. Nobody will mind. In fact, other networkers usually welcome newcomers and bring them up to speed.

Doing so is easy. It just takes a calm breath, followed by a leap of faith. If you already know someone in the circle, simply smile and nod to acknowledge that you're joining their company. When the current speaker comes to a natural lull, you should follow up by extending a hand and introducing yourself. Share a bit of history, explaining how you know your buddy.

If you don't know anyone there, a slightly more heavy-handed segue will be required, but the result will be the same. Here are some examples:

"Mind if I jump in on this? What are you guys talking about?"

"Sorry to interrupt but I overheard you talking about..."

"Hey, great party, huh? I don't believe we've met. I'm Dan."

As a warning, I would suggest not hijacking the conversation the moment you join. This will come off as rude and disgruntle those who weren't quite finished with the previous topic. As long as you don't do that, nobody will mind you participating. If you've been listening politely beforehand, know you can add value and don't interrupt whoever was talking first, there should be no problem.

OFFER TO PAY

This tactic won't be an option for everyone, particularly if you're working on a shoestring budget. However, if you can afford it, offering to pay for a round once in a while can give you an air of generosity, or at least avoid you looking like a sponger.

It's a strategy I use as much for my own integrity as my image. For example, once a year, I meet a group of friends who own a large self-development company. I've bought their courses because they are fantastic and we get on well together. As thanks, if we go for lunch, they always offer to pay. They have the money and they're happy to pay.

Pretty sweet deal, right? Well, yes, but I'm always conscious of not wanting them to think that I only talk to them for a free ride. The truth is, I believe in what they do, I like hanging out with them and I would continue to pay for their work even if they didn't buy me food and drinks. To show that, I combat this dilemma by occasionally getting a round in at the bar to cover some of the meal cost. That way they break even, and our friendship is realigned as a two-way street.

Many authors offer to pay for drinks if they want advice. This is good practice because it shows you appreciate your peers' time. You should never avoid paying or – worse still – expect them to pay because you think they've got more money. For a start, you don't know their financial situation. Secondly, if they really are as successful as you believe, their time is valuable. A drink is a small price to pay for their knowledge.

Lose Yourself in the Celebration

Mastering the techniques we've explored should make it easy for you to enter any event and quickly start mingling. It shouldn't be too difficult after that to find plenty of friends. You'll be circling the room, meeting new faces and collecting business cards with the best of them.

Inevitably, even if it takes patience, you *will* find a person who gets you and your work. Shoptalk will become real conversation and true friendships will blossom. It's okay if you deviate from business. Networking is more about people anyway. Business comes as a by-product of great relationships.

What you're doing here is building friendships that have strong business foundations. If you do it well, people will think of you whenever collaborative opportunities arise. All you need is to be liked and respected and that outcome will be achieved during the course of the night.

Don't worry about getting a little crazy. Where I live, in the UK, we're known for our drinking culture. Adults often bond over a beer or cocktail. It's not the healthiest choice of beverage, nor would I recommend it for anyone with dependency issues or anyone who is below the legal drinking age. But it *does* lower barriers and nurture bonds in record time.

Try not to embarrass yourself but don't worry about the odd slipup because most people won't notice anyway. The other attendees will be far more focused on overthinking everything *they* said the next day as they nurse a hangover. If anything does get noticed, you can always laugh about your mistakes together when you next meet – hopefully, in the morning. This camaraderie is yet another accelerator for building strong relationships.

Actions to Take

If attending afterparties and other additional events:

- ✓ Freshen up and eat between the end of the conference and the beginning of a party
- ✓ Ditch the day's formalities and bring the party
- ✓ Find the organiser to fast-track your introductions
- ✓ Learn to conclude conversations politely so you can meet a range of guests
- ✓ Try to meet people you've talked to online to deepen your relationships
- ✓ Avoid a wallflower mentality by inserting yourself into conversations
- ✓ Offer to pay sometimes to show respect for other attendees' time, especially if they're successful
- ✓ Lose yourself in the celebration because making innocent mistakes together creates camaraderie

13

Late Conference Tactics

It's the last morning of a multi-day conference and you're already exhausted. By now, you've seen the vendors, know many visitors by name, covered every inch of the venue and nailed the main meetings on your agenda.

What now? Have you finished?

Well, not exactly. Conferences are an endurance sport and you must become a marathon champion if you want to squeeze as much value out of the experience as possible. By now, you should be relaxed, unfazed if people see you lounging on the floor in a corner whenever you need to massage your ankles. If you're anything like most attendees, you'll be achy and more than a little fuzzy from a mild hangover. Fortunately, most people will be in need of a nap at this point, which is good because it's one more thing you have in common.

At this point, your primary focus should be on nurturing that common ground. That is why, in this section, we will cover strengthening relationships in the latter stages of a conference.

Do Your Homework

Even if you researched other conference attendees when you first booked your ticket, it's worth trawling the hashtags and groups again, now that you know more names and faces. Generally, a second pass breathes fresh life into a networking strategy, exposing treasure-troves that weren't apparent the first time.

Honestly, I'm not even subtle when I do this. You'll often find me pulling out my phone and asking a writer to spell their pen name for a Google search. Doing this isn't rude. If anything, it shows you're interested. Also, if you follow the Amazon charts as religiously as I do, you'll sometimes recognise their work, which gives you more to discuss.

As they say, knowledge is power, and the more knowledge you absorb, the more connections you can make. If you're not comfortable reacting to book covers and reviews in front of the author, you can always wait until they visit the toilet. This isn't shady behaviour. You can almost bet they're scrolling through a list of your books the moment they leave your company.

Who Do You Know in the Room?

If you've been at the event for over 24 hours, you've probably come into contact with more faces than many other visitors. This is because, while events can be spread over several days, not everyone attends every day. New authors and entrepreneurs turn up each day. Just as you were on day one, they're lost, they know no one and they're looking for a friendly face to help them make connections.

You can be that person.

One of my go-to lines I say to unfamiliar faces whenever I meet them is, "Who do you know in this room? Perhaps I can fill in the gaps." Depending on that person's response, my next line is either a suggestion or a request.

"You know David? Wow, you need to introduce us!"

Or:

"You write thrillers? Let me put you in touch with my friend Jo. Her thrillers are getting a lot of attention at the moment."

By offering to put them in touch with someone first, you're proving that you're open to helping them and they will appreciate that. If it turns out that they're unfamiliar with the surroundings but are actually a hotshot connector themselves, that's great. They can introduce you to someone you haven't thought to approach yourself.

START INSIDE JOKES

Strong friendships consist of shared memories. Spend every weekend with someone and you won't notice how often you reference the past but a random encounter with an old school buddy highlights exactly how much you rely on inside jokes. Usually peppered with sarcasm, these jibes sound offensive from an outside perspective but are ultimately received in good humour. They stick around, even if you haven't seen someone for years.

Remember this popular wisdom:

> "When you fall over, friends ask if you're okay. Best friends laugh, mock you... and then ask."

You won't be able to replicate that sort of connection overnight but you can start building a similar dynamic with friends you've spoken to several times over a multi-day event. I wouldn't go for the throat immediately but I would test the waters from as early as your second encounter. The odd witty remark can quickly evolve a formal business relationship into a full-blown friendship. Just remember not to alienate new joiners who might not have attended the first few days when your in-jokes developed.

FOLLOW UP ON QUESTIONS

Had a burning question the previous day but didn't manage to ask it before someone "borrowed" your new contact? Now is the time to have that conversation. Not only will the extra touchpoint make you more familiar, but the interest shows that you were listening and are the type to seize opportunities.

You can even go as far as asking your new contact if you can take notes as they walk you through a concept over lunch. That way you won't forget their great advice and can carry out their instructions the moment you get home. Plus, there's the added benefit of having something to thank them for on social media after the event.

Don't Gossip

Humans have gossiped for millennia to share awareness of threats and form close bonds with their tribe. It's psychologically rewarding. However, I do *not* recommend you do this under any circumstances in the networking world. Chances are, if *you* are gossiping with someone, they probably gossip about *you* elsewhere. Of course, you want to come up in conversations when you're not present, but not in that way. Gossip will only award you a scandalous reputation in the long term.

But that's not the only reason you shouldn't gossip. Not only is it unprofessional but it can also backfire in unexpected ways. According to a study referenced in *The Happiness Project* by Gretchen Rubin, people associate you with the descriptive words you use to describe others. This association, no matter how illogical, is an interesting insight into the human brain because we can reverse-engineer it to work in our favour.

To give you an example, I've heard the following comments at conferences:

"Sure, she writes 10 books a year but I've taken a look and the writing isn't great. They clearly need to be edited."

"All of his marketing advice is so basic. Really, he got lucky: right place, right time."

Once I'd learned about this phenomenon, I considered what I thought about the people being described. The truth was, I admired them. They were successful and worked hard. That was why they came up in conversation in the first place. It was just that, as with any successes, they inspired jealousy.

In contrast, I analysed what I thought of the people giving these opinions. The first person didn't write 10 books a year. The books they had written weren't reviewed any more favourably than the author they were criticising. Therefore, what I subconsciously took from the conversation was that *they* couldn't write 10 high-quality books a year. My brain made the jump that they either lacked work ethic or writing ability.

Similarly, the author bemoaning a peer's huge success despite only giving out "basic" marketing advice only taught me that they themselves couldn't make that advice work. Hence, they lacked the technical ability or hadn't committed to educating themselves properly. I came to the conclusion that they were projecting their own inadequacies.

Both critics conveyed the opposite of what they intended. Rather than coming across as superior, their gossip did more to shape my perception of them than their rivals.

If you are going to gossip, do so in a positive way. Praise your rivals for their work ethic, meticulous quality and creative flair when they're not there because, if nothing else, it will also improve your public image.

ASK PROBING QUESTIONS

Society tells us not to talk about money, but everyone *should* talk about it, not because of nosiness but because comparing notes can fix so many problems: what works, what doesn't, and how much everything affects your bottom line. It's not about learning how much money a person has; it's about learning *what* they're doing that drives their results.

Networking events feature a lot of showboating. That means it can be difficult to work out who is a success compared to who *looks* successful. Therefore, probing questions come in handy.

I'm not suggesting you lead with one. To get a positive response, you need to build rapport first. I've done this several times, mostly in the later stages of a conference. Times when you can have a casual conversation with a close contact without being overheard often lead to the best answers.

However, to ensure your curiosity doesn't tarnish your relationship, it's useful to allow your questionee an escape route. Try something along these lines:

"Do you mind if I ask you a probing question? It's fine if you don't want to answer."

It's a risky way to start but at least it prepares your conversation partner so the following question doesn't put them on the back foot. As long as you show an earnest intention to learn from their answer and definitely not gossip, most people are happy to oblige. This is where you get the behind-the-scenes details and reasons for their strategy that they would never share in a public forum. Some are even more forthcoming than necessary and will disclose personal information that fully contextualises their decisions.

A few years ago, I spoke to an author who had seen considerable success. The previous year, they had mentored an up-and-comer who had since surpassed them using what appeared to be an identical strategy. Thus, after building rapport, I asked:

"What did your apprentice do that you didn't?"

Admittedly, it was an indelicate question, but it was relevant and would provide insightful results. Was it dumb luck? Or was there a fundamental difference in their plans that most people would never get to see?

Had I been told to mind my own business, I wouldn't have pushed the matter – advice I would encourage you to follow. If they don't want to tell you, that's fine. Drop it and change the subject.

This time, the question was answered calmly and generously. As I suspected, outside appearances were not as they seemed. While the mentee benefited socially from more exposure, they did so by negotiating a deal with a distributor that took a large portion of their profits and limited their creative control. As you can see, the details were more interesting and nuanced than simply stating the student had surpassed the master. Had I not asked, I would never have encountered these potential trip hazards that I can now anticipate and prepare for in my own career.

If you're asking probing questions then you should respond honestly in return. Many authors clam up at this moment, particularly if they're ashamed of how little they've achieved by comparison. However, this is a mistake. Exposing the weaknesses in your own business will create a sense of kinship between you and your confidant. In some situations, it can reveal solutions to some of the issues you face, especially if the other person knows how to take your work to the next level.

Whether or not you get this far, always remember to stay positive. People don't like to expose their secrets and be vulnerable. So, no matter how they answer, always respond positively. Support their decisions. If they worked well, commend their success; if they didn't, remind them that it was a valuable learning experience. Either way, thank them for their time and honesty. Whatever you do, don't share what they told you unless you have their permission.

OFFER TO MEET AGAIN

Visitors move constantly at hectic conferences. Depending on the time and purpose of the event, you could be anywhere from a bar to a beach to a busy auditorium. All the while, you'll be meeting new people and having fragmented conversations, frequently cut short before they get to the interesting part.

If this is your experience then know that others feel the same. With all the options dividing their attention, they might appreciate a moment to have a proper in-depth chat. Hence, that's an opportunity to invite specific contacts that interest you for a coffee and a change of pace.

Nearing the end of a conference, you can afford to be more liberal with your time. You will have spoken to most of the vendors and attended the best talks, so you can afford to meet a newfound friend, even if that means leaving the building in search of a more tranquil spot. This break can provide an opportunity to have an undisturbed conversation with a contact you think shows promise.

COPING WITH A CONFERENCE DISASTER

After packing up, you will leave a conference with an overwhelming haze of opportunities to pursue. Depending on how you've handled yourself, you could also have a healthy dose of post-meeting anxiety.

Did I say the wrong thing to that distributor?
Was I too drunk at that afterparty?
Did I make an ignorant remark during that interview?

All are valid concerns. I felt the same way after making my first ever podcast appearance. At events like these, where you need to fill lulls in conversation, there's a pressure to talk constantly that puts you at risk of saying something you think is witty without thinking through how it could be misinterpreted.

That's a common concern. The whole experience leaves you re-hashing conversations in your mind long after they happened. Thankfully, there's evidence to suggest that lots of people share this concern. Bestselling children's author Anthony Horowitz, who has made hundreds of media appearances, once tweeted that he didn't actually agree with *anything* he said during one radio show interview. The pressure to fill the silence just caused him to spout words without thinking. Post-event anxiety is a monster none of us can escape but one we must learn to ignore.

In more extreme cases, where you've embarrassed yourself so badly there's no coming back, it's helpful to remember that these things happen. A drunken mishap or an off-colour joke too close to a microphone happens on occasion but, unless it makes national headlines, it's unlikely to ruin your career.

Most intelligent people who already know you will realise that the slip-up was an innocent mistake and will forgive you. And anyone who's offended enough to shun you completely would do so eventually anyway. Getting on the wrong side of their wrath was only a matter of time.

The publishing industry is fairly incestuous. Lots of prominent authors know each other and many editors and executives work for several competing publishing houses during their careers. However, turnover is high. That means even the worst reputation will fade as new faces replace old hands. The best strategy is to hold on and endure until the storm subsides.

REALISE WRITERS AREN'T FAMOUS

An added comfort to remember if you've had a conference disaster is that writers aren't famous. Not *famous*-famous compared to other celebrities. When you live and breathe the industry, it's easy to forget this because you see the big players on every stage, blog, podcast and social media platform.

You might know the top 50 authors in your genre by name but readers couldn't identify Dan Brown or James Patterson in a line-up. Ariana Grande, Kevin Hart and Leonardo DiCaprio would get mobbed in a crowd but what about Suzanne Collins, Stephanie Meyer and Jeff Kinney? Respectively, they wrote *The Hunger Games*, *Twilight* and *The Diary of a Wimpy Kid*. They're about as high-profile as an author can get without also being a TV celebrity, yet would a reader recognise them? Would you?

This shows just how little authors matter to the average reader. They don't care about your personality, your scandals, or your rivalries. Their primary concern is whether your books are entertaining and satisfy their needs. As harsh as that sounds, it's a comfort. It means that, no matter how badly you mess up, the news will never reach most readers. And if it did, they wouldn't care.

Actions to Take

In the later stages of a conference:

- ✓ Research the other attendees a second time now that you know more names and faces
- ✓ Offer to connect latecomers with people you've already met
- ✓ Start inside jokes to deepen bonds with new buddies
- ✓ Follow up on questions you've been meaning to ask but didn't get a chance earlier in the conference
- ✓ Don't gossip if you want to be viewed positively
- ✓ Ask your mentors relevant probing questions that they would never answer in a public forum
- ✓ Grab a coffee with promising contacts and finish any incomplete conversations
- ✓ Know the industry is forever changing so a conference disaster won't ruin your reputation with everyone
- ✓ Understand that writers aren't as famous as other entertainers so scandals rarely reach readers

14

Follow-Up

There are two types of authors: those who leave a conference exhausted and those who charge home, energised. No matter what category you fall into, you need to overcome one final, necessary hurdle in the days following a buzzing conference.

The follow-up.

Creating a big splash at an event is fantastic but it means little if you don't connect quickly with your new acquaintances. If you don't follow up while you're fresh in their minds, those leads run cold and forget you.

The brain flushes unused information to save energy. Remember how you used to use a scientific calculator every day at school? Try using one a year after you graduate and you'll see that you've forgotten half the functions. It's a simple machine you used every day, yet the information is gone.

It's like that with people too. Share an office with someone for months and you get to know them well. Spot them out of context at a supermarket a month after moving jobs and suddenly you can't place their face. A year later and you both can't remember each other's name. If you've only known someone for days at a conference, the effect is amplified.

Not following up quickly enough can blur a potential contact's memory of you. The longer you leave it, the worse it gets, so it's best to follow up quickly, preferably in many places. In business, they call this the seven touches of marketing – the idea that someone has to see a product or brand seven times on average before they recognise and trust it enough to buy. Only, in this case, the thing they need to buy is you.

While marketing experts now theorise that people need more than seven touches thanks to the internet's effect on the brain, the concept hasn't changed. It's just become a bigger challenge. The key is to be everywhere. Your audience won't notice you at first but over time they'll grow accustomed to you and feel like they've known you forever.

So how do you start the seven touches without seeming like a stalker? The key is to be subtle. It's not easy but this chapter will help you lodge yourself firmly in the minds of your peers.

COMMENT ON THE EVENT

Every event these days comes with a Facebook Page or hashtag where attendees can discuss everything from speakers to travel arrangements. However, only a fraction of commenters use that strand to its fullest potential after the event. This is the easiest place to begin tying together your online and offline personas, converting real-world contacts into online friends.

A good way to start is by writing a simple post, thanking everyone for their generosity (and tagging them in the message so they know you are mentioning them) and complimenting the organisers for putting on an interesting line-up. The exposure will attract further friend requests and follows.

Share Your Selfies

Lots of attendees take selfies with influencers and authors they admire during large events. Many post these on the internet as they happen. I would suggest, however, holding back until a day or two after the event. That way, you can strategically post them when you get home and tag high-profile attendees you met in your posts, hitting them with another of your seven touches. Psychologically, doing so extends the event in their mind, magnifying their perception of time spent with you.

A bonus of waiting is that your contact will be more likely to have good internet access at home. They would be in a better position to accept friend requests and share posts that would otherwise be missed when they only had access via their phone.

Read Business Cards

Business cards contain lots of information but not always enough to remind you who their owners were and what you discussed. I've made the mistake of waiting days to return to a wad of cards only to discover that I couldn't remember why I owned some, and I missed opportunities as a result.

Not every author writes full-time so some end up handing you a card that seemingly belongs to someone else entirely. "Sebastian Drinkwater" who said he wrote fantasy at the bar might be down as Martin Bradshaw. Why Martin? Well, he did mention it briefly but you've forgotten that Sebastian Drinkwater is his pen name.

Distributors, editors, agents and publishers can be equally confusing. They sometimes hand you their boss's card if they don't have their own, or if they've run out. If you notice when this happens, asking them to write their name on the card can help to avoid confusion. However, that doesn't always happen.

Little tripwires like this have led me to tackle stacks of business cards as soon as possible. I suggest you do the same. To stay organised, I create a spreadsheet with a row for each new contact, documenting their information, plus extra notes on how we know each other. That way, you can ditch the cards in favour of a more comprehensive and searchable record.

Support Your New Allies

The beauty of the publishing industry is that your fellow authors aren't your competition. They can be, if you close yourself off, but the collaborative nature of our work means you can choose to make them more like colleagues. And the more cheerleading you dish out, the more social karma you'll bank, especially if you've met each other in real life.

Knowing these authors intimately will make you want to see them do well – and *vice versa*. Often, the help you can offer conference allies when they launch their next book will attract reciprocal generosity. All you have to do is set the example and others will follow.

Plan a Reunion

No matter how long an event lasts, you are unlikely to complete every conversation on your mind. Don't let the end of the event stop you. You're not intruding if you contact a new friend directly. Most people *want* to network so there should be no issue, as long as you don't expect more value from the relationship than you offer.

If the event didn't give you enough time then a reunion is a good solution. This can be either one-on-one or as a small group. Some authors set up monthly clubs so conference buddies can stay in touch, rather than waiting another year.

Alternatively, you could replicate the in-person experience by using a video-chat service like Skype or Zoom. Both services work well because they allow you to elaborate on ideas more emotively on camera than in an email. They have recording capabilities too, so you can save conversations instead of having to pause to take notes.

Finally, you could organise a same-time-same-place reunion at the conference the following year. Confirming you're attending in advance can persuade others to go again and spark a community atmosphere. That way, you can walk into a room that already contains friends, which will make it seem like you know *everyone*. Imagine how that makes you look to new visitors looking for a someone to show them the ropes. Ultimately, reunions are about strengthening existing connections to become a fixture in their lives. Done well, it can truly enrich your networking experiences.

Many writers I know have used this strategy to great effect. Action/thriller author Steven Moore has organised to meet with conference friends a month or so after first talking to them at conferences. Likewise, fantasy and non-fiction author Sacha Black has partaken in city breaks with other authors, deepening relationships she established months before in formal settings. The options are only limited by your budget and imagination.

ACTIONS TO TAKE

To make the most of your meetings after the event:

- ✓ Use the event's Facebook group or hashtag to thank the organisers and your fellow attendees
- ✓ Attract connections by making your social media presence more visible to other attendees
- ✓ Share your selfies with high-profile guests to level-up your public image and attract more contacts
- ✓ Support your new allies to turn rivals into colleagues and collaborators
- ✓ Plan a reunion to strengthen the bonds you have worked hard to create

15

Building Your Networking Momentum

An author buddy of mine recently told me about his rise to success in a London bar. He had been an author for years, working a day job while making around $500 a month in royalties. That was until 2015, when he released a book that changed his life.

He told me that, instantly, the game changed. His career reached a tipping point and the back catalogue he had struggled to sell suddenly started selling based on his breakout book's success. One month he made $500, the next $23,000, then $36,000, then $49,000. Suddenly, he was making more money per month than he had made all year at his day job.

Overnight, everything became easier. Everything he touched turned to gold. Each new success elevated his reputation, giving him yet more to leverage. Since that initial boost, he has rarely seen a month with anything lower than a five-figure income.

He told me this story because, at the time, I was struggling. I had put in the work, had seen some success but was wondering if the "big break" would ever come for me. Now, I still haven't seen numbers anywhere close to his but I have seen some subtle shifts in my career that, upon reflection, show promise, allowing me to boost my public profile and my income.

Barely a month after that conversation, two event organisers approached me. One wanted me to talk on a panel about social media for authors and the other wanted a 45-minute talk on writing horror. Not too long after that, a podcaster asked if I would like to be interviewed as an up-and-coming writer. The interview would be streamed thousands of times across YouTube, Stitcher and Spotify.

None of these speaking opportunities were solicited. I didn't win a contest or pester the organisers. I didn't pay my way in. All I did was stick to a consistent networking strategy.

In many ways, you can draw a comparison between this occurrence and the one described by the author I mentioned. After years of chiselling, the dam fractured and I was suddenly getting more opportunities for less effort.

That's how it is with networking. Momentum does happen but, for a while, the gains are so small you can't see them. Then, one day, out of nowhere, you notice the ground shaking beneath you as everything snowballs. And as long as you don't stop, the pace just keeps building.

I've certainly seen the work get easier over time. You find yourself surrounded by people and opportunities more often. People that once eluded you suddenly have more time. After a while, they start asking if *you* have time for them. As you become more influential, your reputation starts networking on your behalf.

The conversations change. "You want to give a speech? We'll see. What's your name again?" turns into: "Hey! We've got an event going on this summer. Would you mind delivering the keynote?" Having spoken to people who have transitioned from one to the other, they all credit persistence and momentum.

This chapter will outline strategies that can help you build momentum on your networking success. They are simple and are verified by authors who see great success.

KEEP SHOWING UP

Hollywood mogul Woody Allen once said, "80% of success is just showing up." And he was telling the truth. People fail for a lot of reasons but a common one is giving up. They're not blocked out. There isn't some event that forces them to stop. They just shift their priorities because it makes their life easier if they give up on their dream.

Meanwhile, others maintain their progress. They keep chipping away, writing, getting up early, signing books and paying for advertising. They keep learning, adapting and automating whatever they can to work more efficiently.

Often, dreamers who haven't succeeded complain about the "luck" of break-out stars. Meanwhile, they ignore the work ethic it took for those stars to achieve their dreams. Sci-fi author Justin Sloan isn't a household name but he does live a comfortable life with a full-time income from his books. Yet, he revealed to his Facebook friends in 2018 that he had to publish 40 books before he saw his royalty statements hit a level that meant he could go full time.

It's important to remember this: if you give up without being forced to by some uncontrollable circumstance then you're *choosing* to fail. Succeeding is not something you can control but you can decide to fail.

In creative industries like publishing or broadcasting, when you analyse the trajectory of the big names you see a common pattern: their careers can be tracked using a graph with a long tail of consistent hard work with no reward, followed by an exponential upward curve. No recognition for years. Then one day their fanbase hits a point of critical mass and word of mouth snowballs. They become an "overnight" success, cast into the spotlight. Nobody sees the toil it took to get there.

In networking, the principle is the same. Few people will notice you for a long time. But the number will grow as you keep showing up. First, they talk *to* you. Then they talk *about* you. Eventually, most people will *know* you. Then, when your name is everywhere, all it takes is one slight push and – BOOM! You explode.

Not every networking performance has to be great. As long as you're there, you're remaining open to opportunities. All you have to do is hold on to the belief that the next encounter might be the one that changes your life.

SET UP GROUP CHATS

Social media has evolved. A decade ago, the focus was on the "social" part. Nowadays, most platforms have moved closer to the "media" side and are course correcting, having alienated their users. Where communities once shared their daily lives, now all they see are sponsored ads. Their friends' posts have been squeezed out of their feeds by paid-for content, so they don't write anything either, knowing their words will be lost.

Twitter has always had this celebrity-focused model, as has Instagram. It works well for them. However, Facebook changed, driven by a hunger for ad revenue, and has had to work its way back to the original community model that made it successful.

While the social media titans correct their errors, the best way to get your voice heard now is to create small groups. Messaging apps work perfectly in that regard. Facebook Messenger and WhatsApp have come up trumps precisely for their group-chat capabilities. In these apps, each post is presented chronologically and everyone sees them. Nothing is suppressed to make room for paid content.

As a result, many people favour Messenger over the regular Facebook platform for communicating with friends. It works equally well for keeping up with friends and close contacts. Grouping people who know each other means you can organise when and where to meet when you're all *en route* to the same event and it ensures you never miss one another.

Slack is another great app that many creative entrepreneurs recommend. However, it is targeted specifically at collaborators working on a shared project rather than for regular conversations. Slack has extra functionality for file-sharing and searching. Plus, it enables users to sort chat information into topics, which makes working on interlinked projects easier to follow.

These chat models can be far more effective than public-facing social media sites at helping you to keep in touch with the people who matter most to you.

Maintain the Seven Touches

The seven-touches strategy really works as long as you remember that this number is higher for online marketing. However, it requires persistence. Getting in all seven during one week is unlikely to achieve your desired outcome. This is because the brain typically doesn't retain information long term that is administered over a short time period. To be remembered, you need a longer-term strategy.

Just look at pre-exam cramming. Those who cram their heads full of algebra in the final days before an exam can pass. If they're inherently smart, they can even get a great mark. But studies reported by *Science Daily* and the BBC have shown that crammers lose most of what they learned within weeks of completing the test. Meanwhile, students who build and reaffirm their knowledge over months retain more.

This teaches us a valuable lesson. While being *everywhere* for a week might seem to be a good idea, it's not sustainable and doesn't generate the desired result. Contrary to popular opinion, making one or two appearances every month for years is a better option.

Be a Talent Scout

Reading and talking favourably about your peers' work will stoke the fires of your relationship like nothing else. Make no mistake, I don't advocate recommending everyone to your audience, regardless of quality. But if you read something you think they'll like, sharing your enthusiasm for it will keep your readers engaged and will make you firm friends along the way.

However, your research shouldn't stop there. Deepening relationships is a good plan but isn't sustainable. People retire, they stop writing and they die. To stay on top, you should always be watching the horizon for new talent.

Fortunately, one benefit of regularly visiting events is being primed to spot promising newbies. They're usually easy to spot because they exude tenacity, enthusiasm and intelligence. And you can use those qualities to judge their writing without reading it.

I say this because those who work hard to master one area of their lives often dominate others too. Queen's Brian May became an astrophysicist; athlete, Michael Jordan, became a successful entrepreneur. Overachievers have an intrinsic curiosity and grit that they carry from one passion to the next. They appear to be talented but their real superpower is discipline, which they can apply to any subject.

So, keep a lookout for well-read amateur writers who can hold their own in conversations. If they are committed to learning the trade, they have probably also committed to writing well. Checking out their work will expose exactly who to network with next.

They might not have a lot of clout yet but that doesn't matter. Self-publishing means hard workers aren't held back by publishers' schedules and dreams can be made in record time. Fantasy author Yumoyori Wilson used that advantage to write 60 books in 18 months and it completely changed her life.

Likewise, traditional authors can see similar success if they have a brilliant book and a proactive publisher. Rapid release is less likely but a lot of time and money is focused on debut novels in the traditional publishing ecosystem. That means an unpublished author you meet today could be a household name in six months. Being friends with tomorrow's stars just requires identifying them early in their career.

VARY YOUR EVENTS

Rural networking circles, or those that exist as small, community-driven ventures, tend to overlap little with their corporate-run, urban cousins. At least, that's what I've found here in the UK. For that reason, we will refer to these smaller gatherings as local events, even if they do sometimes occur in cities, to avoid confusing them with slicker, urban operations.

Some authors prefer local literary festivals that are typically lesser-known, whereas others reside exclusively in corporate-funded, city conferences like Frankfurt Book Fair or FutureBook Live. While local events are centred around the joy of authorship and community, urban ones tend to favour creative entrepreneurship and attract an international crowd. Though both are fun and the writers that attend take their writing seriously, you can't ignore their different approaches to creativity.

For the best results I recommend visiting both. That way, you can build a stable, local network and fanbase, while simultaneously making powerful, metropolitan connections. This two-pronged approach allows you to test your social skills in two distinct environments. Plus, the progress you gain in your local area (if you don't live in a large city) will keep you motivated to tackle the more daunting and competitive challenge of the world stage.

COLLABORATE TO GROW

James Patterson changed the game. He is almost consistently the world's highest-earning author, only occasionally being dethroned by J K Rowling and the odd freak release. In 2013, the year E L James's *Fifty Shades* trilogy exploded, earning her $95 million, Patterson came a close second with $91 million – a number he has maintained while she faded. You can't deny it: like his work or hate it, Patterson has grown and maintained considerable momentum.

In part, his writing style plays a major factor in his popularity. So does his history as a marketing executive. However, what has really set him apart from the rest of the bestsellers is his ability to have a constant – and growing – presence in the charts.

Know how he does this?

Collaboration, and lots of it.

Patterson produces upwards of 12 books a year thanks to working with co-writers. As he's already a huge name, most become *New York Times* bestsellers, hitting number one before his last release has slipped from the top 100. His momentum is relentless and he achieves it consistently.

First he writes a 60-page book outline. Then a co-writer fleshes it out to over 300 pages, cutting his workload per book dramatically. He has to project manage his collaborators and edit what they've written but that still means working less than doing it all himself.

Self-publishing has developed this idea further. Many top indies, like sci-fi writer Michael Anderle, create their own fictional universes in which lots of their characters from different series co-exist.

If you aren't familiar with the idea, in the context of story licensing, a universe is a singular fictional world that is inhabited by characters from one or more franchises. These characters can share a storyline but that isn't essential as long as their stories all share an overlap. The theory behind it is that the characters could meet, like every Marvel hero, even if their storylines never cross.

Mirroring the Marvel model, where movies tie together and characters appear in each other's stories, some influential indie writers create multiple entry points into their fictional universes. That way, they are able to funnel readers from one series to another. Once they grow a fanbase using this strategy, they allow lesser-known authors to write stories in their universes. These "smaller" authors get to make money writing a series in an already popular world. At the same time, they grow their own reputation and fanbase. Meanwhile, the "big" author receives a share of the royalties and gets to put their name on extra books, in some cases, adding three or more books a *week* to their catalogue! Their symbiotic relationship allows both authors to move forward.

Now, you might ask two questions:

1. What makes you think I want a part in this business model?
2. What does this have to do with networking?

Well, answering the first question isn't easy because everyone's different. If you're a new author, your aim probably won't be to dethrone Patterson. You might not want to ride the coattails of a big author like him either. Some writers want to write their own books and control their own world, and that's fine.

Patterson's business model is fascinating, though, because it shows that even juggernauts need to network. He continues to add collaborators like J D Barker to his roster to help him test new niches and delight new audiences. You might assume that the "small" author in this scenario is almost always a personal friend but you would be wrong.

Urban fantasy author Elaine Bateman (E G Bateman), who recently secured a deal to co-write a series with Michael Anderle, told me that she had never met Anderle before she got the gig. Initially, she offered to help his business partner Craig Martelle moderate 20BooksTo50K, a popular Facebook group which Anderle and Martelle run together. That's how she got onto their radar. She didn't actually meet Anderle for the first time until much later at a networking event in Bali where, armed with a manuscript, she proposed a shared project. Bateman has admitted herself that this was a massive gamble that cost thousands and only worked because Anderle liked her writing. Despite the odds, though, it paid off! And many authors are succeeding with similar tactics.

Collaboration is a balancing act. If you're willing to give up some creative control in exchange for networking opportunities, it's something to consider. Whether you collaborate to expand your catalogue or to work with a titan, collaboration can help you grow your career, knowledge and reputation.

FOCUS ON DIVERSITY OVER SIZE

A good way to build a strong foundation is to build friendships in various places. You don't need a large network to be successful, just a diverse one, full of people with different skills, connections and areas of expertise. That way, you can use your friends to access second-hand contacts outside your immediate network with little extra effort.

Think of it this way: there are only so many hours in a day. You could spend that time wrangling a hundred bloggers working in niche areas or you could focus on two influential ones and mention their names if you ever need to grab another's attention. Harnessing this idea can cut your networking time to a fraction without stunting your reach.

Of course, the tactic of building relationships with only a few select figures in distinct areas of expertise isn't perfect. Everyone needs a backup in case someone you rely on disappears. That's why I recommend at least two per speciality. The more the better really. But most people, myself included, don't have the mental bandwidth to maintain more than a handful of relationships.

By finding and focusing on two contacts in each field (blogging, editing, cover design, publicity, etc.) you will end up with a diverse portfolio to run your business and survive if someone disappears. More connections will provide more stability, but networking with this minimalist strategy helps you to avoid working harder for diminishing returns.

ORGANISE AN EVENT

Remember that tip earlier about how you should seek out event organisers because they know everyone? Well, the reason they know everyone is because lots of people have the same instinct, particularly at smaller, local events where the organisers are easy to recognise and approach. Lost in unfamiliar surroundings, the first thing many travelling writers do is look for a familiar face. In most cases, that's the person who brought everyone together.

The reason is simple: even if visitors have never met you, as an organiser, you are a landmark that proves to them they're not lost. They're safe. People talk to you because they know you're there to guide them. You can introduce them. You can help. There's no ambiguity as to why you're there. As a result, you are the go-to contact for fresh faces and special guests alike.

Knowing this, it makes sense to be that person. Now, I know what you're possibly thinking because I've had this doubt myself:

I don't have the credentials to set up an event. Don't you need authority?

Running something for the first time does feel like being left in charge of scissors without adult supervision. Only, you *are* the adult supervision. You just don't realise it yet.

I discovered this revelation after helping to organise a local book fair as part of a previous job I held as a publishing assistant. 20 authors turned up, alongside 250 readers. The event didn't change the world but it was definitely considered a success. I've spoken about it to other organisers who manage similar operations.

You know what they had in common? Doubt. They all felt they lacked the clout needed to bring together such an event. However, in each case, they found that they didn't need clout. It would have helped but the demand was already there. Everyone just waiting for someone to stoke the fire. Once they attached a few names to the project, leveraging them to attract more recognisable guests was easy.

If managing a fair or conference isn't your *forte* but you still want the benefits, you can always approach an existing organiser and offer to help. Stretched thin, they are always happy to have someone take a portion of their workload. That could involve taking over the social media, or even ushering attendees through the right entrance on the day.

There are plenty of ways to attract the kudos attached to being an organiser. All you have to do is make the first move.

Create a Safety Net of Professionals

If you run a publishing team with tight deadlines and launch targets then compiling a single dream team of collaborators won't always be enough. Editors, proofreaders, designers, publicists, other professionals – they can all disappear. Life is complicated and sometimes it happens. And while knowing a master of each discipline is fantastic, they are little use to you if you suddenly find yourself missing a player.

You can, potentially, delay a launch while you find a replacement or wait for them to return. Indies and traditional publishers alike do this on a regular basis. Readers might express disappointment but they'll wait. It's not the end of the world. Online retailers, however, can be far less forgiving if you've already set a pre-order deadline. Their policies can mean losing royalties and even having your pre-order privileges revoked, which can ruin future release strategies.

That's why, if you do choose to set a pre-order date at bookstores before you have the final book ready, I strongly recommend networking with multiple experts in each discipline. By sharing work between several freelancers, you'll open yourself up to more opportunities while safeguarding your business against the threat of no-shows. If it means having to wrangle an extra few contacts, the extra conversations will be worth the heightened peace of mind.

AIM FOR THE BACK ROOM

One way to step up your networking efforts is to gain support from the establishment. We have already reasoned that the majority of networking doesn't actually resemble old men making deals in elitist wood-panelled clubs. Nowadays, it has become accessible to everyone.

Nevertheless, that sort of thing does still happen, mainly between traditional publishers and retailers but increasingly between powerful indies and tech companies. They are as much a part of the establishment today as Penguin Random House, HarperCollins and Barnes & Noble due to the vast proportion of the market they control.

Not only do tech companies take a cut from indie author sales but also from the traditional publishers – in ebook, print and audio. They have also leeched huge percentages of the global market share from traditional retailers. Amazon controls over 50% of the total US book market and Kobo has global sales of over $14 million a year, a figure which is set to grow since it has partnered with Walmart.

I first noticed their growing influence in 2017 at The London Book Fair when a few prominent indies mentioned a restaurant situated near the back of the venue called The Club at the Ivy.

It's a bar open only to paying members or invited guests. They use it as a place to hold private meetings.

At the 2018 event, a friend of mine mentioned that he had been invited for a meeting there so, interest piqued, I took a closer look. While I couldn't get past the security at the door, I did glimpse inside. Olive-green leather, wood panelling, brass plaques as placeholders – it was a Dickensian cliché. Another world, reserved exclusively for the industry's most powerful publishers, literary agencies and tech companies.

Many of the prominent tech companies in this space certainly wouldn't have had reservations a decade ago. Apple Books (then called iBooks), Barnes & Noble's Nook and Kobo all started in 2009. Google Play wasn't even launched until 2012! Yet they're so integral as distributors these days that they're impossible to ignore. That doesn't mean these back rooms will disappear, or that Silicon Valley or Asia's tech giants will force out traditional publishers in place of tech-savvy author-clients. Publishers will just evolve to master ebook and digital audiobook marketing. Once that's done and they find new ways to entice successful indies onto their client lists, their decline will hit a plateau. In short, they will adapt and survive so it's worth getting an insight into their world.

That's not to say you should immediately scout out an equivalent club at every major book fair and pay for membership. Like all networking venues and groups, not all back rooms hold equal value. Thus, a better approach would be to find a connection in your existing network who has attended your local back room and enquire about its worth. If the conversation goes well, you might find that they even have the authority to invite you.

Pay to Meet Industry Leaders

One of the publishing industry's greatest qualities is that is has low barriers to entry. While you can spend thousands on producing and launching a book, it *is* possible to start on a shoestring budget. That's what makes it so exciting. The bestseller dream is open to everyone.

Although, cash injections do often separate how successful authors can be after their books start to sell in numbers that are commercially notable. While some writers prefer to stick to their shoestring origins, others opt for more expensive options. $100 stock-image covers and $200 ad campaigns can evolve into $1,000 character photoshoots – complete with a live model – and $5,000 book trailers.

The bigger you get, the more luxury you can afford until you can practically bulldoze your way onto bestseller lists. Not everyone wants a billboard on Times Square but those who can afford to can have it (that's $1.1 million to $36 million per year, in case you're interested).

In some respects, networking is similar. I realise this isn't easy to read as someone who isn't yet seeing massive success. It needs to be mentioned, however, in case you have deep pockets and haven't thought to explore this avenue.

It's possible to become well-known and meet creative thought leaders without spending cash but money *can* fast-track your social climb. In essence, it can grant you access to some of the industry's best advisors – those who are attuned to market trends and can help you identify emerging opportunities.

Pre-2012 self-published authors were innovators. They saw the future of ebooks and struck gold when most writers were turning up their noses. The early adopters made millions, without professional covers, simply because there was less competition.

Similarly, advertising moguls like Mark Dawson and Nick Stephenson pioneered using Facebook ads to sell books online. They now live jet-setting lifestyles of fame and fortune.

Some innovative romance and crime writers thought to set their books and series in one universe. They did this to cross sell their series to readers, knowing that they were more likely to buy books in multiple series if they were set in a world they already knew and liked. Toby Neal did this with her *Paradise Crime* series which is still hitting bestseller lists years after she launched her first book. Likewise, Marie Force's *Gansett Island* series has turned into a $10-million-a-year empire while sci-fi author Michael Anderle is well on his way to replicating this success with his *Kurtherian Gambit* series.

After these innovators explode their careers, they don't stop innovating. If anything, they work harder to reinvent themselves by networking with other innovators to figure out their next move. And if you want access to this knowledge and foresight then you need to be willing to pay.

"So my *friendship* isn't worth their time?" I hear you ask. Well, no. But don't be offended. It's an economic fact, not a judgement on your character. Industry leaders aren't monsters who think they're better than you. They're just too busy to focus attention on something that won't help them maintain or grow their success.

In the author community, a handful of indies make over $10,000 a day. Say they work 10 hours a day. That means their time is worth $1,000 per hour. It's true that they don't technically work the traditional hourly-rate model because their books sell 24 hours a day and sales vary based on multiple factors. But many report a drop in revenue whenever they stop writing and publishing. They need to write a lot and publish often so their time really is worth that much. That means the 15-minute chat you wanted cost them $250.

You see, those working at the vanguard of their industries don't have "just 15 minutes" to answer questions. Even their tooth-brushing routine has become an efficiency exercise. As a result, the only way to catch their attention is to make it worth their time, by paying for it, or proving that it will benefit a cause they believe in that doesn't require money.

As mentioned, it won't be an option for everyone. However, you might want to consider paying to network if you're doing well but have hit a glass ceiling. $500 is a small price to pay for an hour of one-to-one coaching from a six-figure author.

JOIN A MASTERMIND GROUP

It would be nice to be able to afford one-to-one access to the world's elite creatives. However, there is a cheaper alternative. Millions aren't necessary. In some cases, a few hundred dollars will gain you a 12-month membership of access. Don't close the book. This isn't a sales pitch. I have no vested interest in this game. Just advice.

Mastermind groups are clubs, usually run by a star leader, for ambitious individuals willing to invest in their future. They do this by paying to meet regularly with likeminded men and women. Usually, new members have to have already attained some success to be eligible but that isn't always the case. Any vetting process is done to ensure the other members also get value from meetings.

The benefit of mastermind groups is that you get access to advisors who have already mastered areas you want to tackle. You are encouraged to reciprocate advice, but that's because members are supposed to learn from each other. If you get along and your work overlaps in some way, you can even share contacts for mutual benefit.

These groups come in several tiers. Some require no funds but are typically invite-only. This isn't something you can control unless you know a member and are particularly persuasive. Others I've seen range from $1,000 to over $100,000 per year, depending on the calibre of members. Again, this isn't an option for everyone but it might be for you if you have the funds and drive to propel your reputation.

STUDY AROUND THE SUBJECT

Publishing is a big industry full of diverse professionals. On top of that, it's also growing. As technology and culture evolves, so do the people we need to work with as authors. Over the years, ebooks have exploded. So has audio. The way we consume content has developed and, as a result, we need to network in different circles to stay relevant. Complacency means stagnation.

It is, however, possible to stay ahead by educating yourself to new practices and opportunities. I can't recommend an exhaustive list of resources to check out because it morphs as authors' needs change. But I can provide a list of the primary resources I used when researching the concepts behind this book, and which I continue to use to seek new networking opportunities.

Some of the most helpful books that inspired this one include:

- *How to Win Friends and Influence People* by Dale Carnegie
- *Influence* by Robert B. Cialdini
- *The Go-Giver* by Bob Burg and John David Mann

The best blogs on business and networking for authors include:

- JaneFriedman.com/Blog
- JAKonrath.Blogspot.com
- TheNewPublishingStandard.com
- SelfPublishingFormula.com

And a selection of the best podcasts that explore entrepreneurship and authorship include:

- The Self Publishing Show
- The Tim Ferriss Show

- ○ The Marie Forleo Podcast
- ○ Impact Theory with Tom Bilyeu
- ○ The Creative Penn Podcast
- ○ Self Publishing School

All of these resources cover networking, writing, entrepreneurship and mindset, as well as broader business topics, but they aren't the only ones. There is an ever-expanding library of great resources for you to explore in every format.

PAY IT FORWARD

One common principle in networking is paying forward your success with advice and opportunities for new writers. This is because getting to this point where all authors are respected as "real" authors, no matter how they publish, has taken a mammoth effort. Publishers have historically kept writers in the dark so figuring out their tactics hasn't been easy. However, now that their secrets are exposed, it's important not to repeat that history for our own benefit.

As we end this book on how to achieve more by bringing people together, our attention must turn to legacy. How do you want to be remembered by those you meet? As a massive success who hid their secrets? Or as a generous teacher and connector who left their little corner of the world better than they found it.

Yes, paying it forward means providing lasting value for your whole career. But not only that, it also means being remembered for your work, your character and the positive impact you had on the lives you touched. Start with this in mind and you can't go far wrong.

Actions to Take

To keep building momentum with your networking, you should:

- ✓ Keep showing up because consistency will work in your favour
- ✓ Create group chats on social media to nurture regular communication with your closest contacts
- ✓ Look for more ways to get your seven touches
- ✓ Be a talent scout for rising stars
- ✓ Vary the events you visit to develop local and global friendship circles
- ✓ Collaborate with other authors to grow
- ✓ Develop a diverse network of influencers rather than a large, specialised network
- ✓ Get involved in organising events to become a go-to social figure
- ✓ Create a safety net of professionals to survive if a regular collaborator disappears
- ✓ Find out who in your network has access to elite networking clubs and try to get invited
- ✓ Consider paying to learn from industry leaders
- ✓ Join a mastermind group to share knowledge and resources with other influencers
- ✓ Study around your subject to stay relevant
- ✓ Pay forward what you've achieved to give newer authors opportunities

16
YOUR NEXT STEP

You now have the knowledge you need to start and grow a successful author network. The strategies outlined in this book are enough to start from scratch, with no industry contacts. You should now know:

- o The benefits of networking
- o Places where writers can build a network from scratch
- o How to network with professionals
- o Why being shy or a technophobe shouldn't hold you back
- o How to reach out and make relevant industry connections online
- o How to strengthen those online relationships and build your reputation without leaving home
- o The various places you can meet industry contacts in the real world and how they compare
- o Mental and practical ways to prepare for a physical event

- A clear strategy for maximising your networking efforts at a publishing conference
- A clear game-plan for getting invited to event afterparties and side events
- Manoeuvres that help you circle the room at afterparties and turn contacts into real friends
- Ways to create lasting bonds at the end of a multi-day writers' conference
- Follow-up ideas to ensure your newfound friends remember you beyond the conference
- Connection-building methods that deepen long-term relationships
- Ways to build your networking momentum and become a respected, influential figure
- How to leave a legacy characterised by paying forward opportunities

You are now prepared to execute on a solid networking strategy, avoid potholes and live the author lifestyle you've always wanted. As the ancient Chinese proverb goes, "A journey of a thousand miles begins with a single step." Good luck, and allow me to guide that first step. I know the perfect place to find your first contact and start building a little social karma.

SAY HELLO

You guessed it: it's me.

I know exactly how it feels to start out in this big, daunting industry. You don't have to start alone because I'm here to be your first contact! Reach out and I'll happily respond to emails or answer questions. They can be about this book or any other topic around the author-entrepreneur lifestyle.

The best place to get in touch is to sign up to my email list and respond to my newsletter. To make me a part of your network, sign up at:

www.DanielParsonsBooks.com/Networking

You'll get a free resource that lists the best writer-friendly conferences worldwide, plus dates, locations and other details as a welcome gift to help you form a networking strategy.

REVIEW THIS BOOK ONLINE

Help spread the word by reviewing this book on whatever website you use to get your reading fix. It makes a huge difference to sales and could help bring new authors into the networking ecosystem, which means more opportunities for you. Many readers don't realise the power of good reviews. The more, the better!

RECOMMEND IT TO YOUR FRIENDS

Nothing helps determine the success of a book like word of mouth. If you thought this book was valuable, please tell your friends online or in person.

If you post a great review on Twitter, be sure to use my handle @dkparsonswriter so I can see it and respond. I appreciate the feedback and I'm always on the lookout for writing topics if you have any suggestions.

BE A SUCCESS STORY

The final way you can help is by becoming a success story and helping to make this industry the best it can be. Try new things, work hard to grow, and get in touch. Your success will be a massive indicator of whether I've done my job.

Good luck and happy networking!

ALSO BY
DAN PARSONS

Have you read them all?

THE #ARTOFTWITTER

In *The #ArtOfTwitter*, writer and Twitter coach Dan Parsons explains how he grew an 80,000+ strong army of loyal followers and gained real-world influence as an indie author. Breaking his tactics into short chapters and simple, actionable steps, he demonstrates exactly how any creative professional can achieve similar results.

Whether you're a writer, artist, musician, or any other creative professional, *The #ArtOfTwitter* will show you how to:

- Understand the changing world of social media
- Avoid common mistakes
- Grow your popularity without being suspended
- Gain a bigger audience by using hashtags
- Build strong relationships with your followers
- Nurture follower engagement
- Save time with Twitter apps
- Implement a strategy for sustained growth
- Make money with Twitter marketing
- Ensure every tweet is a hit
- Get real-world influence

THE DEAD WOODS

When Will and his friends decide to spend one last night together after graduating university, none of them realise the danger that lurks in plain sight. At first they're having fun, caught up in the thrill of running through the forest, firing Nerf guns at under-paid zombies-actors. Then that all changes when darkness falls.

It quickly becomes apparent that the actors are very good at what they do. Too good. Armed with only an arsenal of Nerf guns, the group quickly figure out that they'll need more than just foam bullets and sandwiches to get them through the night.

LAST CRAWL

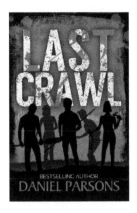

Milo's fear of everything has held him back for as long as he can remember. He knows university will drag him out of his comfort zone but he has no idea just how uncomfortable he is about to become. When zombies strike during his first night out on campus, he quickly discovers that making friends is a matter of life and death.

A chance encounter reveals that zombies don't attack extremely drunk people. Can Milo and his new flatmates band together to survive the most dangerous bar crawl the world has ever seen?

THE WINTER FREAK SHOW

After twelve-year-old Toby Carter escapes a brutal workhouse at Christmas, he can't believe his good fortune. Adopted by a band of travelling performers called The Winter Freak Show who put on spellbinding shows each night, he finally believes he's found the family he always wanted. Then everything falls apart.

Children are disappearing throughout the city. Pretty soon, all evidence points to those Toby trusted the most and he finds himself caught up in a conspiracy far more sinister than he ever imagined. Defenceless and on the run, he's confronted with two options: uncover the kidnapper before another child falls victim or stand by and watch as the shadowy criminal becomes unstoppable.

The fate of Christmas rests in the balance.

FACE OF A TRAITOR

It's been a year since thirteen-year-old Toby Thornton found his long-lost family. But already cracks are appearing in his dream life. Forbidden from seeing his magical friends at The Winter Freak Show, he begins to realise how much he misses adventure. So when he gets word that the elves are in danger, that's all the excuse he needs to run away from home.

It isn't long before he discovers that things are worse than he imagined. Nicko has been kidnapped. And without the ringmaster's guidance, his elves have descended into chaos. A band of shapeshifting enemies lurk among their ranks. Monsters are on the loose. And the secretive mastermind behind it all is trying to resurrect the most frightening evil the elves have ever faced. Only Toby stands in their way.

If he fails, forget Christmas. This time, the human race will fall.

BLOTT

Thirteen-year-old Blott Meritum has hidden his freakish ability since he was a toddler. However, as his people hurtle toward starvation, he has no option but to risk exposure and take action.

He commits a forbidden crime to save his people, and soon discovers that the world outside the village harbours unexpected perils, and that his ability means he can change his people's whole existence. However, a sinister voice inside his head has other ideas.

Will he keep his humanity and save his people? Or will he be consumed by the monster inside him?

About Dan

Dan Parsons is the author of eight books, three of which are international bestsellers. His non-fiction work includes two instalments in his *Creative Business Series*: *Networking for Authors* and *The #ArtOfTwitter*. Under the name Daniel Parsons, he has written fantasy and horror novels, including *The Twisted Christmas Trilogy*, *The Necroville Series* and *The Canvas Chronicles*.

His work has hit bestseller lists in the US, UK, Canada and Australia. In 2017, he saw his debut novel become the fastest downloaded children's book in North America on Christmas Day, four years after publication. On top of that, his zombie story *The Dead Woods* (then *Necroville*) was named one of Wattpad's Top Zombie Stories, and was used to promote Hollywood's *Pride and Prejudice and Zombies* movie.

Besides writing and publishing, he has worked for three traditional publishing houses, and as a bookseller for both an independent bookshop and a high-street chain.

He loves talking to readers and writers alike and can often be found at literary festivals and conventions.

To contact Daniel, sign up to his bi-monthly newsletter at www.danielparsonsbooks.com/networking, check out his books online or join his 80,000+ Twitter followers. He loves hearing from readers.